Unpaid work in the household

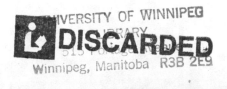

Women, Work and Development, 1

Unpaid work in the household

A review of economic evaluation methods

Luisella Goldschmidt-Clermont

Published with the financial support of the
United Nations Fund for Population Activities
(UNFPA)

International Labour Office   Geneva

ISBN 92-2-103085-7
ISSN 0253-2042

First published 1982
Third impression 1985

Printed in Switzerland

PREFACE

In 1976 the World Employment Conference, when stressing that "freely chosen employment enters into a basic needs policy both as a means and as an end", recalled that, in particular, employment "yields an output" and "provides an income to the employed". In so doing, it was, no doubt rightly, placing emphasis on remunerative employment and on market-oriented outputs rather than on unpaid work in the subsistence sector or production for direct household consumption.

It is clear, however, that the household sector, the value of whose production has been estimated at 25 per cent to 40 per cent of the measured Gross National Product in industrialised countries, plays an extremely important role in satisfying many of the basic needs of the population and that this role is undoubtedly even greater in developing countries with their large subsistence sector. There has therefore been increasing interest in assessing the value in economic terms of the goods and services produced by households for their own use or consumption, as a contribution to measuring and, therefore, providing a basis for understanding some of the ways in which the market and non-market sectors interact, and the impact of these interactions on real household incomes and welfare.

Most of the attempts to impute values to unpaid work carried out within the household for the benefit of its members have been made in industrialised countries in the context of highly monetised economies and societies. A number of different approaches have been used. The present study examines these approaches, the difficulties met and the strengths and weaknesses of the results they yield, while an Appendix provides summary descriptions of some 75 evaluations and their results. This analysis leads the author to suggest further lines of research in this area. This is indeed a field deserving further investigation, both in developed countries and, subject to testing and adapting methodologies as appropriate, in the developing world as well. The present study provides a useful starting point.

Antoinette Béguin

Assistant Director-General,
International Labour Office.

Acknowledgements

This research project was supported partly by a research grant from the Fonds National de la Recherche Scientifique, Brussels, and partly by the International Labour Office.

My gratitude goes to Richard Anker, Antoinette Béguin and Peter Melvyn for encouragement and support received since the early stages of the study.

I also want to thank K. Brehmer, F. Mehran, N. Phan-Thuy, J. Royer and K. Walker who read the first draft of the manuscript and made constructive comments.

I am indebted to P. Gualtierotti for her contribution to the bibliography and for securing many documents, to the ILO Central Library staff for its co-operation and to the Stanford University Library for giving me access to its collections.

Any correspondence relating to this monograph should be addressed to the Population and Labour Policies Branch, Employment and Development Department, ILO, Geneva.

Luisella
Goldschmidt-Clermont,

Centre d'Economie Politique,
Institut de Sociologie,
Université Libre de Bruxelles.

CONTENTS

CHAPTER 1

Introduction

In the face of difficulties experienced by industrialised market economies in reducing unemployment, considerations on the future of work focus on alternatives implying the spreading of existing employment opportunities among a larger number of persons, and a correlative redistribution of time between employment and free time. In such circumstances, individuals would be faced with wider choices than presently on the allocation of their non-employment time between education, training, leisure and unpaid work geared to production for self-consumption. The latter, unpaid productive activities, include housekeeping, vegetable gardening, do-it-yourself repair and construction, child care, etc.; they constitute the household sector of the economy. Interest in the household sector is therefore growing, although relatively little is known about its interrelations with the market sector.

Production processes occur without discontinuity through the market and household non-market sectors of the economy. The transformation of natural resources, e.g. agricultural products, into goods ready to satisfy human needs is a chain of successive production processes which do not change nature when passing the borderline of monetary exchanges. Unpaid work in the household still transforms and distributes, i.e. adds "value", to products bought on the market before they are physically consumed. The borderline between production and consumption, as drawn in economics, is only a conventional line, convenient for distinguishing between relatively easy to measure monetary transactions on the one hand, and non-monetary production for exchange or self-consumption on the other.

The similarity between production processes occurring in the market and in the household is further underlined by the overlap between the two sectors: children are cared for, food is prepared, the ill are nursed, etc. as a result of paid and unpaid work inputs. Interactions between the two sectors are continuous: transfers of manpower from the household to the labour force (e.g. when former full-time homemakers take up wage employment and reduce their work inputs in the home); transfer of production from the household to the market economy (e.g. when the same former full-time homemakers spend part of their wages in buying, on the market, goods or services they were producing previously); and, inversely, transfers from the market sector to the household. Although such interactions have been observed and to a certain extent analysed, the underlying mechanisms are not well documented. Why, how, when do these transfers occur? What do they mean in terms of personal standard of living, of economic growth, of social and economic development? How do market rigidities affect these transfers? What would the impact be, for instance, of a reduction of working hours on the labour supply, on the production of goods and services for self-consumption, on the consumption of market goods, on time available for leisure, education, etc.? A better understanding of the relations between the household sector

1

and the market sector would have something to contribute to answering such questions.

One prerequisite for the analysis of the economic interactions between the market and the household or, in other words, for the analysis of their interface, would be the existence of common units of measurement. In the market sector, however, production is usually measured in value i.e. in monetary units, while, in the household, available measurements are most generally expressed in time units. Economists have therefore translated time units relative to household production into value units, by assigning a monetary value to unpaid work in the household.

In this study, we review several economic approaches to the evaluation of unpaid work inputs in the household. The emphasis is on methodology. The specific economic conditions prevailing in household production are considered in relation to those prevailing in market production. The impact of labour market and of household constraints on labour power transfers between the household and the market are kept in mind as well as the role of personal and social value systems.

This review leads us to point at the need for a complementary approach if the dynamics of market vs household production are to be better understood. Such understanding of the dynamic interactions between the market and the household can be of use, in industrialised societies, for interpreting historical and forthcoming trends in the transfer of labour power and of production between the two sectors, and for the formulation of welfare policies. It might also prove useful for the effective use of manpower resources in development planning, particularly in relation to the role of women in development.

CHAPTER 2

Objectives and Methodology
of the Study

2.1 Scope and Limits

Since the earlier days of national accounting, economists have been concerned with the delimitation of what is and what is not to be accounted for. One of the simplest rules i.e. accounting only for goods and services produced and distributed in the market sector, was broken right at the start as imputations were made in national accounts for agricultural product consumed by the farmer himself. Concern was expressed, and in some cases solutions were found, for other products and services which do not pass through the market such as the services received from owned dwellings (for which therefore no rent appears in the market), voluntary work for the community, time devoted to study or, more recently in welfare assessment, for the value of leisure time. The most longstanding concern has, however, been for the value of "housewives' services", which are considered the largest single item missing in national accounting.

By focusing on unpaid work in the household, this study covers a broader range of activities than "housewives' services" which are only part of household productive activities along with "do-it-yourself" household repair and maintenance, vegetable gardening, etc. On the other hand, the scope of our study is narrower than others, as it is limited to productive activities carried out by household members for consumption by their own household, i.e. we leave out other unpaid productive activities such as voluntary work for "consumption" by other members of the community.

It is by now largely undisputed that non-market household production is an economic activity, sharing many characteristics with market production, and linked to the market as, for instance, in decisions relative to time allocation between paid and unpaid work. It is, however, also recognised that imputing a value on household production, no matter how desirable, meets with difficulties which have so far prevented inclusion of this item in national accounts. These difficulties arise from the lack, for household production, of direct market transactions which, for similar goods and services produced in the market, determine a socially accepted value, a price.

Economic evaluation attempts have been made, for national accounting or other purposes. In chapters three to five, we review about 75 economic evaluations of unpaid work inputs in the household, or of their counterpart, non-market household output, and discuss them from the methodological angle i.e. according to the method of value imputation. These evaluations are summarised in the appendix where they are listed in chronological order.

Only estimates relating to industrialised societies were retained for this review.

Even within such a limitation, coverage is probably incomplete and contributions for filling gaps would be welcomed. The conclusions arrived at probably apply, to a large extent, to developing economies although an additional study might prove necessary in order to examine specific aspects connected with societies presenting a lesser degree of monetarisation.

As the objective of this study is to discuss economic evaluation methodology, and not the value (absolute or relative) of unpaid household activities, no attempt is made at comparing evaluation results. The values are, however, given in the appendix summaries, as an indication of the orders of magnitude at stake in household production. Readers interested in such comparisons are referred to Hawrylyshyn (1976) who has compared about 14 evaluations, while making adjustments for differences in scope (definition of what is being measured, i.e. housewives' services only or all household members contribution, etc.) and for differences in imputation basis (wages, before or after taxes, etc.), and to Murphy (1980) who reviewed about 40 evaluations.

There is no general agreement as to what should be measured, nor as to the method of measurement itself, particularly as both items are likely to vary with the purpose of the evaluation. Scope, method employed and purpose of the evaluation are reported in the appendix summaries, and are left, as much as possible, in the authors' own wording. An analysis of the discussions on what is economic and therefore to be measured would carry us out of the boundaries of this study. In order, however, to clarify at the outset what the evaluations discussed are broadly about, we will give, as a point of reference, M. Reid's definition (Reid, 1934, p. 11) which we consider, in practice, closest to most other definitions implicitly or explicitly used :

"Household production consists of those unpaid activities which are carried on, by and for the members, which activities might be replaced by market goods or paid services, if circumstances such as income, market conditions and personal inclinations permit the service being delegated to someone outside the household group."

As a "test which may be applied in order to separate production from consumption and social activities", Reid proposes :

"If an activity is of such a character that it might be delegated to a paid worker, then that activity shall be deemed productive."

Again, for clarification purposes at the outset of this study, we may indicate that, to-date, two out of three of the macro-economic evaluations situate the value of household production (grossly defined as above) somewhere between 25 and 40 per cent of the accounted for gross national product of industrialised societies. This gives a rough indication of its order of magnitude in monetary terms.

2.2 Typology of Unpaid Work Evaluation Methods

If non-market (household) and market processes are to be compared, common units have to be found for expressing them in comparable terms. Such units may measure volumes or values, of inputs or of outputs.

Volumes. Volumes of work inputs, in the household and in the market, can be assessed in terms of labour power involved in the process (number of workers) or of

4

work-time absorbed (hours of work). Volumes of other inputs (raw materials, equipment) or of outputs can be expressed in physical units of goods or, in the case of services, in number of persons cared for (children schooled, meals served, patients' days in hospitals, etc.). The relative importance of market and non-market production can then be assessed, but the comparison betwen the market and non-market sectors can only be carried out where the units are similar, i.e. function to function.

Values. Values for processes occurring in the market can readily be assessed, as it is conventionnally accepted to equate value and price for economic measurement purposes. If a product has no price, i.e. is not sold to the consumer (e.g. public administration services), the convention, in national accounting, is to account for it at the value of factor inputs (wages and capital services).

Household economic processes occur outside the market pricing mechanisms; to achieve comparability between the two sectors, a monetary value has to be imputed on non-market processes. It is common practice to impute on non-market goods and services the value of similar goods and services available on the market; this method applies, for instance, to agricultural product consumed directly by the producing farmer. Market values can thus be imputed on household work inputs or on household product. Imputation on the basis of the value of capital services was considered but not pursued because of the difficulties it raises (Hawrylyshyn, 1977, pp. 92-94).

Value imputations for household work inputs have usually been derived from market wages. The basis for the imputation can be any of the following :
- wages of substitute workers who could be hired for performing productive activities in the household; these substitute workers can either be polyvalent (domestic servants, housekeepers, family aids) or specialised (cooks, laundresses, baby-sitters, etc.) :
- wages of workers performing, in market enterprises, functions equivalent to household production functions;
- wages of workers performing in the market sector, tasks requiring qualifications similar to those required by household tasks;
- wages forgone in the market by those engaged in unpaid household work, i.e. opportunity cost of time;
- average wages of market workers, sometimes differentiated by sex, age, education, residential area, etc., or legal minimum wages;
- wage in kind, i.e. non-cash benefits (housing, board, clothing, medical care, etc.);
These wage-based imputations in some evaluations are applied to the number of workers involved in household production, while in others they are applied to the number of work-hours devoted to household production.

Value imputations for household outputs can be made at the market consumer-price either of a global replacement for the household product (e.g. care of infants, of the ill, of the aged in institutions) or of a replacement for a specific household product (a meal away from home, a shirt washed and ironed in a commercial laundry, a pound of commercially prepared jam, etc.). The value of specific household outputs has in some cases been derived from consumer expenditures for related inputs in raw materials and equipment.

The framework just outlined will be used for presenting the evaluations reviewed in this study. This framework differs in two manners from the classification adopted in

**Table 1 : Typology of Economic Evaluation Methods
related to Unpaid Household Work**

Object of measurement	Expressed in	Imputation basis
Volume of Input		
volume of work inputs	workers or time units	
volume of inputs other than work, i.e. goods consumed in the production process	units appropriate to the activity	
Volume of Output		
i.e. goods or services produced	units appropriate to the activity	
Value of Input		
value of work inputs	monetary units	
		wages of substitute household workers polyvalent or specialised ;
		wages of workers performing in market enterprises functions similar to household production functions ;
		wages of workers performing in the market sector, tasks requiring qualifications similar to those required by household tasks ;
		wage forgone, i.e. opportunity cost of time ;
		average wages of market workers or legal minimum wages ;
		wage in kind, i.e. non-cash benefits.
Value of Output		
i.e. goods or services produced	monetary units	
		price of a market replacement of household product ;
		related consumer expenditures.

Hawrylyshyn's earlier review (Hawrylyshyn, 1976). First, Hawrylyshyn is concerned exclusively with monetary evaluations, particularly in relation to national accounting, while we are considering a broader spectrum of evaluation methods. Secondly, even for monetary evaluations, we tend to depart from Hawrylyshyn's analysis and to enter into finer distinctions if economic circumstances justify it. For instance, because of differing labour productivity between the household and market enterprises, we distinguish between wages for performing a function in the household and wages for performing the same function in a market enterprise, while Hawrylyshyn discusses the corresponding evaluations in a single category.

Table 1 summarises the typology used in the subsequent analysis of economic evaluation methods related to household unpaid work. The evaluations themselves are summarised in the appendix.

2.3 Aspects of the Interface between the Market and Non-market Sectors

Before proceeding with this review and without going into the details of an economic theory of household production vs market production, we will make explicit a few considerations underlying our analysis.

Constrained work capacity allocation. In industrialised societies, individuals dispose of a certain amount, however limited, of choice in allocating their work capacity towards the satisfaction of their needs or wants. They distribute their work capacity between market and non-market activities according to complex strategies which, besides having economic interest, take into account social and personal values, and which are constrained by environmental circumstances.

The increasing monetarisation of the economy which has accompanied industrialisation and urbanisation is experienced at the household level as a need for cash income which can only be secured through market related activity. Time-use studies, however, show that non-market economic activity absorbs a share of human work capacity of the same order as market activity (3.1.1). An amount of both market and non-market productive activity seems to be indispensable to household functioning; at least a minimum of work capacity has to be allocated to both.

Limited substitution between market and non-market work. Although a certain amount of substitution between market and non-market activity is possible, both sectors introduce constraints which limit substitution. To take only one example : some forms of employment, particularly those which, in addition to wages, carry social security and other benefits, can only be secured if one offers sufficient guarantee of supplying a certain number of hours of work within a defined time schedule ("lumps" of hours) and with continuity over a certain time span. On the other hand, non-market productive activities may require relatively large work inputs at irregular, sometimes unforeseeable intervals (fruits and vegetables have to be picked and preserved when ripe, an ill household member has to be nursed), or they may require relatively small work inputs, but at close intervals (e.g. meals usually have to be available three times a day or more often with young children) which break up the remaining time in portions not usable in employment. Several modes of social organisation have been devised, tried and, to varying degrees, are in operation to meet this difficulty. One of these modes of social organisation which is perhaps the most widespread, is to assign individuals different roles in market and non-market production, according to age and sex.

The market and non-market sectors, therefore, appear related to the extent that labour substitution and production substitution are possible between the two. But the relation is altered when the limits to substitution set by the two sectors' rigidities are reached. In addition to these economic considerations, the impact of social and personal values which further restrain substitution possibilities, should be taken into account.

Labour productivity and value of time. Under limited substitution, the two sectors operate in related but distinct conditions which affect their relative competitiveness and equilibrium, and bear on their respective labour productivity and value of time. To take again one example : if, because of social values or labour market rigidities, an individual is constrained to assign all of his/her work capacity to non-market activities, he/she may find it economically or socially rewarding to perform not only the most productive activities, but also to use his/her available time on activities which are less productive, or would even be considered sub-productive by market labour-productivity standards.

In addition to limited substitution considerations, differences in the circumstances of production in the market and non-market sectors should induce great care in imputing monetary values from the first to the second. The first is the kingdom of monetary accountability with its rewards for economies of scale, for investments in labour saving equipment and the discontinuance of "less productive" (i.e. less rewarding in monetary returns) labour intensive activities. These "less productive" activities, if essential to the functioning of the economic system, may well find themselves transferred to the non-market sector. For instance, some distribution functions are transferred from the market to the household with the expansion of self-service and out-of-town shopping centres, which require an increase of households' inputs, i.e. time of more qualified household members, private transportation, physical handling of goods purchased, private storage, etc. In contrast, the household furnishes personalised services and operates with low overhead costs and no distribution costs, a situation placing it at an advantage for labour-intensive activities.

Externalities and quality of life. The non-market sector partly operates in non-monetary circumstances ; its real output is valued simultaneously in economic, social and personal terms. The result may be a somewhat foggy perception of its own economic circumstances, with, perhaps, the exceptions of a greater sensitivity than the market to externalities and to quality of life considerations.

Need for economic evaluation of non-market sector. We argue, therefore, that care has to be taken when imputing values and when studying the relations between the market and non-market sectors. We share, nevertheless, with others the opinion that, notwithstanding the difficulties involved, it is necessary to assess the economic and social importance of the non-market sector for the sake of a better fundamental understanding of industrialised societies, and for the sake of policy implications.

8

CHAPTER 3

Unpaid Work Evaluations based on Volumes of Inputs or of Outputs

In this chapter, evaluations based on the volume of inputs are considered first, followed by those based on the volume of outputs. Conclusions are then presented relative to these two groups of evaluations.

3.1 Evaluations based on the Volume of Inputs

Volumes of inputs in household production can be assessed in number of workers involved, in work time absorbed or in goods consumed in a productive activity. The first two relate to the volume of work inputs, and are discussed in 3.1.1; the latter relates to inputs other than work, and is discussed in 3.1.2.

3.1.1 Volume of Work Inputs

Number of workers. In an assessment of the economic contribution of homemakers in 1929 United States, H. Kneeland bases one of her approaches on the labour power involved. The number of full-time homemakers is compared to the number of persons, male and female, in the labour force (Kneeland, 1929). A similar approach is used for Hungary (Matolcsy and Varga, 1938) and the United States (Reid, 1947; Kyrk, 1953). (*See appendix for summaries of evaluations, and bibliography for full references*).

Work time inputs. Attempting an evaluation of the order of magnitude of household production in relation to overall United States economic activity, L. Goldschmidt-Clermont compares the number of hours worked in the market sector against those worked in households (Goldschmidt-Clermont, 1952). The same approach is used by : Dayre calculating the global national workload of France (Dayre, 1955), H. Fürst comparing the relative order of magnitude of household and market productive contributions in the Federal Republic of Germany (Fürst, 1956), J. Fourastié, for France (Fourastié, 1965), J. Morgan et al. evaluating economically productive work done for purposes other than monetary rewards in the United States (Morgan, Sirageldin and Baerwaeldt, 1966), H. Schulz-Borck in the Federal Republic of Germany (Schulz-Borck, 1975) and Adret evaluating the relative share of paid and unpaid work in France in 1975 (Adret, 1977).

The above mentioned evaluations differ in mode of data collection (gross

9

estimates based on Census data interpreted in different ways, time-use surveys differing in data collection methodology, etc.) and in scope (all household unpaid work or only full-time housewives', etc.). They are therefore not strictly comparable and cannot be used for intertemporal comparisons. At the macro-economic and household levels, the evaluations quoted in the preceding paragraph show, for the countries concerned and at the dates indicated, a number of hours of work in unpaid household work of the same *order of magnitude* as in the overall market sector. This result is not too surprising; given labour market constraints and household work requirements which limit their opportunities for alternative work, housewives not in the labour force (the main contributors of unpaid work in the cited evaluations) tend to devote to household work what is socially accepted as a work day (probably not unrelated to the length of the work day in the market sector).

In this section on volumes of work inputs, the review was limited to time-use research oriented towards the *evaluation* of household production expressed in time units. Other time-use studies, utilised in evaluations expressed in monetary units, are mentioned with the corresponding evaluations in the appendix summaries. An extensive review of time-use research would be out of the scope of this study. (For a review of time-use studies in relation to household production, see Walker and Woods, 1976.) However, two results derived from time-use research, dealing with the variations over time of unpaid work inputs in the household, will be mentioned here. The first is relative to their variations over the life-cycle, variations mostly reflecting changes in family composition or, more precisely, in number of children and age of youngest child. The second is relative to historical trends. Detailed time series permitting reliable comparisons over long time spans (several decades) are missing. There are, however, indications that household unpaid time inputs decrease, but at a slower rate than has often been expected. Some may want to see in this trend a Parkinson's law effect: work expands to fill available time. There are, however, also objective factors to explain it: higher standards of living (cleanliness, hygiene, care of children), reduced number of household members participating in household work (e.g. the decreased role of children themselves as a result of longer schooling), the transfer from the market to the household of certain tasks (e.g. a share of transportation, of consumer goods distribution, of household repairs and maintenance), externalities related to urbanisation and industrialisation (e.g. increased need for housecleaning and for laundering resulting from air pollution). These factors partly offset others working in the opposite direction such as improved housing conditions and equipment, transfer to the market of certain productive activities formerly performed in the household (particularly in the field of goods production), etc. In the resulting balance, what are the respective shares of a Parkinson's law effect (to meet social norms or, perhaps, a psychological need for self-justification), of a socially or personally desired increase in the standard of living or of an increase in the household workload imposed by the economic organisation? These questions would be worth some further research, particularly on behalf of those interested in welfare assessment and policy formulation.

An evaluation method, measuring work time in order to assess output by function, was introduced in household economics by J. Warren (Warren, 1938 and 1940) in the United States . J. Warren adapted the "work unit", an agricultural productivity measure which scaled amounts of widely different kinds of output into units of time required for their production. On the basis of a time-use study, she identifies the task-specific variable that appears to be most closely related to the time spent on the task, and computes the average time spent on it ("work unit") under average household conditions defined according to this variable. E. Wiegand (1953), K. Walker (1955 and 1958) and S. Manning (1968) pursuing this approach with more comprehensive time-use data, isolate the specific variables that exert the greatest influence on the amount of time spent on six household tasks accounting for 4/5 of household work inputs, and compute the corresponding "work units" or "predictors of time costs" (Manning). For instance, time devoted to meal preparation appearing to be mostly influenced by the complexity of the meal served, six types of meals are defined incorporating varying number of dishes and using varying degrees of commercially prepared ingredients; average times for preparing them are computed. G. Gage (1960) bases her monetary evaluation of household unpaid work on these work units, while B.A. Weisbrod (1961) bases his on a less elaborate "responsibility unit" consisting essentially of the number of household members taken as an indicator of output (see 4.1.1). The "housework study", which is currently carried out in Finland (Suviranta and Heinonen 1980; Suviranta and Mynttinen, 1981) also bases the monetary evaluation of unpaid household work on the combined assessment of volume of output (home care of children, housecleaning) and of time inputs (see 4.1.2 and 5.1).

Finally, K. Walker and M.E. Woods (1976), finding that several variables influence simultaneously the time-costs of an activity, and that the determination of work units raises enormous difficulties, revert to using amount of time per se as a measure of the workload in the household, and of household production itself. They find family composition variables (number of children, age of youngest child, wife's employment status, etc.) to be the major determinants of time inputs, and to constitute therefore an acceptable indicator of the workload and of the volume of household production. Because these family related variables are simple to determine, time averages obtained from sample surveys could be extrapolated without too much difficulty at the aggregate level.

3.1.2 Volume of Inputs other than Work

Inputs other than work have also been used as a starting point from which to assess the relative value of some household production activities in relation to productive processes occurring in the market.

M. Reid analyses United States family expenditures in 1941-42 in an attempt to assess the volume and nature of household production according to household money income and to urban, rural non-farm and rural farm residence. From expenditures, she derives, for instance, data on the ratio of flour incorporated in commercially baked goods purchased by households to flour for home baking. The same procedure is applied to yard goods for home sewing vs ready-made clothes, to laundering at home vs giving laundry out to commercial enterprises, etc. (Reid, 1947). She finds that farm families carry on more household production because of lower availability of commercial goods and services. She also finds that low income forces many families to perform certain productive tasks themselves rather than purchasing the commercial equivalent. Low income, therefore, also explains the higher level of household production among farm families.

11

A variation on this method, relying directly on values and not going back to volumes as Reid does, was used by others at the aggregate level. From increases in consumer expenditures for certain goods and services traditionally produced in the household, it is sometimes infered that the volume and value of household production are decreasing. In fact, such increased levels of consumption also reflect increased standards of living, and may only indicate changes in the *relative* share of household vs market production for the good or service concerned. The market may have taken over a large share of production related to the increase in the standard of living, without, however, suppressing household production.

3.2 Evaluations based on the Volume of Outputs

Evaluations of the volume of household output refer to the good or service produced, in units appropriate to the activity. An example of the kind of result that this approach may yield is given by Fürst's estimate of the amount of transportation service provided by housewives in relation to food preparation. On the basis of the average weight of food purchased by households, she concludes that households, in the Federal Republic of Germany, transported, in 1954, a weight of food equal to the weight of petrol transported by the federal railways (Fürst, 1956).

3.3 Conclusion

In this chapter, evaluation methods were reviewed based on what was characterised as the "volume" of inputs or of outputs in household production, in contrast with methods based on values which will be discussed in the next chapters.

Such volume based methods contribute to one of the goals pursued with non-market production evaluation: the determination of its relative importance to market production, at the aggregate level. This is particularly true of the approaches which express, in number of workers or in time units, the effort directed at satisfying human needs and wants through the market and non-market sectors. Approaches expressing their results in other units (e.g. weights), while giving interesting indications on orders of magnitude for specific production activities, do not lend themselves to all desirable levels of aggregation.

These evaluations contribute to the assessment of the relative magnitude of what happens on both sides of the line separating the market and non-market sectors. If time-series on time spent in market and non-market activities were available, they would provide important information on the shifts from one sector to the other; data collection methodology, however, still needs to be refined and standardised before such time-series can be established. These evaluations do not inform us about the forces pulling or pushing labour power and production from one sector to the other. One exception is M. Reid's study on the impact of residential area and family income on the volume of household production.

CHAPTER 4

Unpaid Work Evaluations based on the Market Value of Work Inputs

In this chapter evaluations based on the market *value* of work inputs, are first presented according to the basis selected by the various authors for their evaluation. They are followed by an analytic discussion divided in two parts: comments relative to all wage-based evaluation methods and comments relative to particular methods. Finally conclusions are presented relative to the whole chapter.

4.1 Presentation of Wage-based Evaluations

Monetary values can be imputed on unpaid work inputs in the household on the basis of market wages or of the market value of non-cash benefits enjoyed as a member of the household. The evaluations discussed in this chapter are grouped into six categories, based on:
- wages of substitute household workers, polyvalent or specialised (4.1.1);
- wages of workers performing in market enterprises, functions equivalent to household production functions (4.1.2);
- wages of workers performing in the market sector, tasks requiring qualifications similar to those required by household tasks (4.1.3);
- wages forgone in the market by those engaged in unpaid household work i.e. opportunity cost of time (4.1.4);
- average wages of market workers (differentiated or not by sex, age, education, residential area, etc.) or legal minimum wages (4.1.5);
- market value of non-cash benefits shared by the unpaid household worker as a member of the household i.e. market value of a wage in kind (4.1.6).

4.1.1 Wage of Substitute Household Worker

The first imputation we are aware of is by Mitchell et al., in the National Bureau of Economic Research investigation on income in the United States from 1909 to 1919. In order to arrive at an order of magnitude of housewives' contribution to national income, they assign full-time housewives the "average pay of persons engaged in Domestic and Personal Service (a group that includes many other occupations besides female domestics), as a conjectural estimate of their services" (Mitchell, King, MacAulay and Knauth, 1921, pp. 58-59).

Polyvalent substitute. Cannon, in 1927-28, interrogating New York State farm homemakers on the rate of pay they would impute on their own work, finds them resorting to the pay of women hired to do the housework (Cannon, 1928). Cannon is concerned that these homemakers give no recognition to differences in skill and in extra effort between housewives and hired domestic labour. Andrews, for 1932 United States, uses wage rates of houseworkers and of housekeepers to estimate the lower limit of the money value of unpaid household labour (Andrews, 1935). The imputation of domestic help wages on unpaid work inputs has been widely used afterwards as an evaluation method for: Sweden (Lindahl, Dahlgren and Kock, 1937); Hungary (Matolcsy and Varga, 1938); the United States (Kuznets, 1941); Finland (Lindberg, 1943); the United States (Reid, 1947); Norway (Norge, 1948); Denmark (Danmark, Stat. Depart., 1948 and 1951); the Federal Republic of Germany (Fürst, 1956); Belgium (Chaput-Auquier, 1959); the United States (Weisbrod, 1961; Rosen, 1974); Finland (Lindgren, 1974); the United States (Brody, 1975); Canada (Adler and Hawrylyshyn, 1978) and the United States (Ferber and Birnbaum, 1980).

Specialised substitute. Many of these authors are concerned with the basis of the evaluation: even for routine tasks i.e. those susceptible of being delegated to a paid worker and therefore being measured (see definition in chapter 2), substitute polyvalent household workers are considered to produce work of lower quality and quantity than housewives. As a response to this concern, other authors impute on unpaid household time, the wages of substitute workers who can be hired to accomplish special activities in the household (cook, seamstress, laundress, baby-sitter, etc.). H. Kneeland, aiming at establishing "a rough and hazardous guess of imputed earnings, ... a lower and upper limit to woman's economic contribution in the home" for 1929 United States, imputes an amount slightly larger than a houseworker's wage for routine tasks, two or three times as large for management and, for other tasks, intermediate values based on wage rates customarily paid for each type of substitute workers. She stresses that arbitrary judgements are involved in the estimate and that it is practically impossible to employ a corps of specialised workers in the home (Kneeland, 1929, pp. 35-38). Imputation of specialised household workers' wages was used as the basis of the evaluation for: the United States (Gage, 1960; Shamseddine, 1968; Pyun, 1969; Sirageldin, 1969); Canada (Lacasse, 1971); the United States (Ruggles and Ruggles, 1975; Kendrick, 1977); France (Kendé, 1978) and the United States (Hauserman and Fethke, 1978). Clarke and Ogus (1978) refer to its use by courts in England, France, the Federal Republic of Germany, the United States, Australia and New Zealand.

4.1.2 Wage for Market Equivalent Function

Perhaps as a result of decreasing availability of specialised household workers who could be hired as substitutes and whose wages could be considered, certain authors adopted as a basis for the imputation, the wages of workers performing in commercial enterprises functions similar to those performed in the household (restaurant cooks and assistant cooks, workers in commercial laundries, nursery school teachers, etc.). In some cases, averages between wages of skilled and unskilled workers in these professions are used.

14

This approach was adopted for: Finland (Honkanen, 1967); the United States (Sirageldin, 1969; Chase Manhattan Bank, 1972; Walker and Gauger, 1973; Brody, 1975); Canada (Adler and Hawrylyshyn, 1978), the United States (Murphy, 1978); the Federal Republic of Germany (Schacht, 1979); the United States (Gauger and Walker, 1980) and Finland (Suviranta and Heinonen, 1981).

4.1.3 Wage for Market Equivalent Qualifications

Awareness of differences in responsibility level and qualifications, between household activities and market equivalent functions, led to considering the wages paid in the market for occupations presenting similar characteristics, rather than for those resulting in a similar product. Job analysis techniques used in personnel management are applied to household tasks to determine occupation equivalences.

This approach was used, although not always pursued to the wage imputation stage, in the Federal Republic of Germany (Stübler, 1967); the United States (Arvey and Begalla, 1975); the Federal Republic of Germany (Schulz-Borck, 1975; Deist-Bohner, 1977) and Switzerland (Bund Schweizerischer Frauenorganisationen und Betriebswissenschaftliches Institut der Eidgenössischen Technischen Hochschule, Zürich, 1981). In the Netherlands, this approach was combined with others (wage of substitute household worker, forgone wage and household composition) to obtain the evaluation (Nederlandse Gezinsraad, 1972).

4.1.4 Forgone Wage or Opportunity Cost of Time

Departing from the evaluation methods analysed in 4.1.1, 4.1.2 and 4.1.3, which are based on the hypothetical substitution of an unpaid worker by a wage worker accomplishing similar production functions, a radically different approach is to impute, on household work time, the wage the unpaid household worker would earn in the market if he/she would choose to give up household work and take up employment. This approach entails a substitution of activity (employment vs unpaid household work) by one person, instead of a substitution of workers as in the previously described methods. It is inspired by econometric research on consumer behaviour and time-allocation. After G. Becker's (Becker, 1965) and K. Lancaster's (Lancaster, 1966) pioneering work in this field, a large amount of research has gone into developing a "household production function" approach to consumption theory. References to this research appear in the bibliography under the names of O. Ashenfelter, G. Becker, R. Berk, S. Berk, J. Cogan, M. Ferber, J. Gerner, W. Gramm, R. Gronau, O. Hawrylyshyn, J. Heckman, K. Lancaster, R. Michael, J. Mincer, J. Muellbauer, M. Murphy, R. Muth, M. Nerlove, J. Owen, R. Pollak, T. Schultz, T. Wales, and others.

The home activity models thus elaborated are based on the assumption that, under specified restrictive circumstances, households allocate time so as to maximise returns. As a result, it is assumed that if a household member works in the household rather than in the market, it is because returns from unpaid household work are perceived as equal or higher than those from market work. Utility derived from the forgone market wage is therefore smaller or equal to utility derived from unpaid

15

household work, and the forgone market wage reveals the monetary value the household places on the allocation of its member's work time to household production.

This evaluation method, which originated at the micro-economic level, was sometimes extrapolated at the macro-economic level. It was used for : the United States (Sirageldin, 1969; Pyun, 1969; Kreps, 1971); the Netherlands (Nederlandse Gezinsraad, 1972); the United States (Gronau, 1973a); Israel (Gronau, 1973b); the United States (Weinrobe, 1974; Gronau, 1976, revised 1980); by courts in several countries (Clarke and Ogus, 1978) and for the United States (Hauserman and Fethke, 1978; Ferber and Birnbaum, 1980).

4.1.5 Average Wages of Market Workers
and Legal Minimum Wages

The imputation raises problems in the determination of a "forgone wage" when the unpaid household worker has no market employment and his/her potential wage is therefore undetermined. As a solution to this difficulty, some authors have used as imputation basis, the average wages of female market workers (evaluation of wage to be imputed to housework time), taking sometimes into account the educational level. Average wages were used for the Federal Republic of Germany (Fürst, 1956); the United States (Machlup, 1962; Nordhaus and Tobin, 1972); Israel (Gronau, 1973b); Japan (Japan, Economic Council, 1973); the United States (Brody, 1975); Japan (Japan, Supreme Court, 1975); Belgium (Kredietbank, 1975). Others have used all workers average wages : Canada (Adler and Hawrylyshyn, 1978). The legal minimum wage was imputed on teenagers' household work time, in 1971 United States (Gauger and Walker, 1980).

4.1.6 Wage in Kind i.e. Non-Cash Benefits

A sixth, rather different method of imputing a wage on unpaid household work, is to consider the non-cash benefits the worker shares as a member of the household, and to equate them with a remuneration for the work performed. This approach was used for 1973 United States by B. Bergmann when trying to estimate what the housewife receives as return for her work : "almost all the pay takes the form of non-cash benefits ... room, board, clothing allowance, medical care, all-expenses paid vacations and the benefits she gets out of her own domestic services" (Bergmann, 1981, p. 83). It should be noted Bergmann is not attempting to evaluate household production per se, but only the housewife's share of returns on work inputs.

4.2 Analysis and Discussion of Wage-based
Evaluation Methods

4.2.1 Discussion of all Wage-based Evaluation Methods

Imputations reviewed in this chapter share one characteristic : household activity is perceived as the production of services, the value of which should be estimated at market prices of labour-factor (input) costs i.e. wages. Other evaluation methods discussed in chapter 5, consider household activity from the angle of the market value of its output.

Apart from differences in the imputation basis, these evaluations differ among each other in several ways: some cover only the household productive activities of full-time housewives, while others cover housework done by all household members, gainfully employed or not (do-it-yourself repair and maintenance are, however, usually not included); the statistical basis varies from a rough estimate of the number of full-time housewives or of housework time costs, to detailed time-use surveys; fringe and non-cash benefits and the incidence of taxation are or are not accounted for in the imputation; etc. Corrections for these differences are required before comparisons can be attempted. Such comparisons between the results obtained through different approaches have been made either by the authors themselves when they tackle the evaluation through several methods or by reviewers (Hawrylyshyn, 1976; Murphy, 1980). The focus of this paper being on methodology, readers interested in the values themselves are referred to the original publications and to the reviews mentioned.

Time-use data. Among wage-based imputations, those requiring time-use data share the difficulties of time data collection. (The more thorough do; others, however, just guess the time-costs of household production on the authors' subjective criteria.) K. Walker, internationally known for 25 years of work in collecting time-use data in relation to household production, reviews the commonly used techniques and concludes that they each have serious limitations (Walker, 1980a, pp. 127-129 and 1980b, pp. 26-32). Among the most intractable difficulties, one finds individuals' limited aptitude to recall past activities and to evaluate the time involved, and the need for the researcher to categorise activities.

Other problems often raised, but which are more amenable to a solution include: the distinction between work and leisure (a problem only because the approach is to impute a wage per unit of time; in approaches based on real output, this distinction is not necessary: leisure can be productive, just as work can be enjoyable), and between production and consumption; the distribution of observed work time between different activities pursued simultaneously (e.g. house repair and child supervision); the handling of on-call time (being available in case of need when a child is sleeping). These two latter problems already were raised by Reid "because they necessitate many arbitrary decisions as to the time spent in various tasks" (Reid, 1934, p. 167); they still receive very different treatment in different evaluations. (See, for instance, Suviranta and Heinonen's (1980) maximum evaluation of child-care time). An accepted practice seems to be to distinguish between primary and secondary activities, and to totally disregard additional activities performed at the same time. Occasionally estimates neglect this distinction; an household member may then be credited more than 90 hours of unpaid work in a week.

Intertemporal comparisons based on the value of work inputs require time-use data; their difficulties are those mentioned above, and are worsened by the need for longitudinal data on wages which are not readily available.

Men-women wage differentials. The division of labour by gender, which in industrialised societies assigns major responsibility to men for wage-earning and major responsibility to women for household production, affects women's earning capacity in the market (lower investments in women's education, employers' expectation that women will show a lower commitment to market work, etc.). This results in women's wages being, on the average, lower than men's. When women's wages are used for the evaluation of unpaid household work, the bias imposed by social roles on their market-wage earning capacity, is reflected on the imputed household wage. Adler and Hawrylyshyn (1978) calculated that in 1971 Canada, household work was worth 41.1 per cent of the GNP on the basis of female wages, and 53 per cent on the basis of male wages. In other words, market factors reduce the value of non-market household production when market wages are used as a basis for the imputation. Women's economic contribution in the market is underevaluated because of their "primary" household role; their economic contribution in the household is underevaluated because of their "secondary" role in the market. The latter is a consequence of the evaluation methodology.

Major labour power shifts. For evaluations at the aggregate level, estimates based on market wages present one further difficulty: they utilise values which are linked to a given labour market and disregard the changes these values would undergo if unpaid labour power moved to paid work. For instance, wages of housekeepers might rise if a large number of presently full-time housewives would seek employment and hire substitutes to do housework in their homes. While the opportunity cost of time of women lawyers might decrease if a large number of trained lawyers, presently full-time homemakers, would enter employment. Evaluations therefore are significant only in relation to a given labour market.

4.2.2 Discussion of Particular Wage-based Evaluation Methods

Discussion of evaluations based on wages of substitute household workers

Basic assumptions. Introduced at a time when the employment of domestic help could be considered a realistic alternative to unpaid household work (according to Stigler, 1946, p. 3, the ratio of servants to private families in the USA fell 36 per cent from 1900 to 1940), imputations based on the wage of a substitute household worker (4.1.1) rely on a certain number of assumptions:

(a) housework *can be* accomplished by hired workers for a wage; when the reference wage is that of a specialised household employee, a further assumption is that housework can be split in separate services to be accomplished by several household workers;

(b) the *resulting product* is equivalent value-wise;

(c) there are housekeepers, domestic servants, etc. *available* to substitute for unpaid household members at the wages and working conditions implied in the imputation.

Tasks susceptible of being delegated. Assumption (a) may, to a certain extent, be considered as satisfied a priori if one sticks to the definition given in chapter 2: the criterion of what part of housework is being measured, is precisely the possibility of

18

delegating the tasks to a hired worker. Specialised substitutes do not however exist for all household productive activities; in this sense, the polyvalent substitute constitutes a more realistic approach.

Assumption (b) is debated by the very authors who base their imputations on wages of substitute household workers. As mentioned above (4.1.1), polyvalent household workers are expected to be less productive, quantity and quality wise, than housewives. This expectation perhaps reflects differences in household work experience between employers (usually experienced homemakers) and employees, who used to be young girls coming from rural areas to the city to earn some money and precisely to gain this experience before marrying and setting up their own household. With the historical trend away from full-time domestic servants and towards househelp recruited among experienced housewives hired on an hourly basis, to generalise the above-mentioned expectation is questionable, particularly if one sticks to the definition, i.e. to tasks which can be delegated. (Housewives' management role is discussed below). Individual productivity differences exist among market workers as well as among homemakers and among household employees, but differences between the two latter categories, as argued by Ferber and Birnbaum (1980, pp. 398-399), need not be systematically in one direction.

For imputations based on specialised household workers' wages, the bias is usually expected to be in the opposite direction. The housewife, termed a "general practitioner" by Ferber and Birnbaum, is expected to be less productive than the specialised cook, laundress, seamstress, etc. who come to her house for wages.

Availability of substitutes. Assumption (c) is not satisfied when it becomes less and less possible to hire substitute workers at the wages and working conditions implied in the imputation. This trend is verified historically in all industrialised economies. Without claiming that economic considerations are the only ones at stake (social status considerations and other social circumstances certainly also play a role in the general disaffection for domestic employment), it seems that domestic wages and working conditions do not favourably compete with other sectors in attracting manpower; and vice-versa, that the expenses for domestic help do not compete favourably with investment in household equipment and market supplied services.

Household workers' wages are usually at the minimum wage level. It may be hypothesised that domestic workers are underpaid in relation to other market occupations as a result either of low labour-productivity in the household (which prevents it from offering wages as high as other sectors do) or of labour exploitation within the household or of a combination of both. Or it may be hypothesised that domestic workers are overpaid in relation to labour productivity in the home, in which case potential employers renounce hiring domestic servants and resort, instead, to labour saving equipment, to commercially prepared products and to commercial services, i.e. resort to a partial transfer of production to the market. In the absence of monetary evaluations of labour productivity in the household compared to labour productivity in the market sector, it is not possible to choose between the above mentioned hypotheses. It is likely, however, that all these factors play a role in the gradual reduction of household employment. In such circumstances, i.e. disappearance of domestic servants and uncertainty as to household labour productivity in real terms vs market labour productivity, wages of household workers appear as a somewhat crude tool for measuring the value of that part of household production which has not been transferred to the market.

For imputations based on wages of specialised household workers, assumption (c) essentially never can be verified: it would be impractical, even if such specialised household workers were available, to hire them for short periods and at time intervals in the same day (preparing, serving and cleaning up meals for a total of two or three hours, at three different moments in the day; etc.). Furthermore, problems of categorisation of time-use data (4.2.1) weigh heavily in this approach where different wages are used as imputation basis.

As a result of this analysis, it appears that imputations based on the wages of specialised household workers are less satisfactorily fulfilling the corresponding basic assumptions, than imputations based on the wages of polyvalent household workers. Although the discussion has pointed at some limitations of the latter approach and at the decline of its validity over the 60 years which have elapsed since its introduction, it remains a simpler, easier to handle wage-based evaluation method, not deprived of logical coherence.

Selection of reference wage. Although the choice of the wage base is more easy in this substitute household worker approach than in other wage-based methods (see for instance below, discussion of method based on wages for market equivalent functions), it is not without creating some problems. For instance, wage rates being higher in urban areas than in rural areas, certain authors have applied lower reference wages for household workers in the latter. As a result, for a same volume of product, i.e. a same output in real terms, the monetary evaluation gives a lower value for farm households than for city households. This, again, underlines the difficulty encountered above (4.2.1) namely the impact of labour market circumstances on wage levels, their repercussion on the evaluation, and the resulting lack of relation between the evaluation and the household's real product.

A similar difficulty arises with the imputations attributing a higher value to time devoted by the housewife to management than to routine tasks. At the limit, a homemaker spending all of her time in management (shopping around for best buys, securing market services) and producing a minimum of goods and services herself would be imputed the highest wage, even if, in the process, she squanders the family income; while a homemaker doing all the work herself (canning, ironing, etc.) and, thereby, saving some of the family's money income, would be imputed the lowest wage. This paradox again underlines the difficulty arising when a wage is imputed which is not related to *real* household output. Such a situation arises because of a fundamental difference between household and business operation. In business enterprises, the economic consequences of poor management will eventually show up in the firm's accounts: the household can function while ignoring its non-monetary input or output flows.

R. Gronau discussing the evaluation method in which "time inputs in home production are assigned the prices [i.e., according to context, the wages] the household would have to pay, had it purchased the services in the market", points out that "these market prices have been explicitly rejected by the household as a true measure of its productivity. The family could have bought the home services in the market but preferred not to do so, either because it found their prices too high, or because it found

20

their quality wanting." (Gronau, 1980, p. 414). Although we agree with Gronau's analysis (purchase on market rejected by the family because too expensive or because of wanting quality) and with part of his conclusion (underevaluation of household product when market product quality is wanting), we do not agree with his conclusion (not a true measure of household productivity) when the market product is considered too expensive. In this case, the household considering the market price, finds it rewarding to perform the service itself; it measures its own real output at the value of the forgone expense, a "high" value; the household does measure its productivity at the market price. In other words, it seems to us that rejection of the purchase on the market, may in some cases point at an underevaluation of the household product by the wage-of-substitute-household-worker approach, but does not infirm the evaluation method in itself.

Discussion of evaluations based on wages for
market equivalent functions

   Basic assumption.   Evaluations based on wages paid for market equivalent functions (4.1.2) assume that the performance of a certain task (cooking, ironing, etc.) commands a specific wage; labour productivity circumstances under which the task is performed are not taken into consideration. This proposition is grosso modo verified in the market sector : wages, output and prices are tied to each other in ways which prevent one of the three going wild in relation to the other two; in the non-market sector, by definition, such relations do not exist. Again, the household can function while ignoring its input-output flows; its real output per work hour may be very different from the output in business enterprises; it may be low without the household "going out of business". To impute a business enterprise wage on household work time regardless of real output, therefore, seems hazardous.

   Selection of reference wages.   In addition, a large range of arbitrariness can occur in the selection of the appropriate market equivalent occupations (functions); some authors do not indicate their selection criteria; others stress the function and/or responsibility level, in some cases using wage averages for different skills and responsibility levels within a profession (e.g. average between senior cook and cook helper wages). Averages constitute to a certain extent a solution for the choice of the wage basis, but not for the productivity problem discussed in the previous paragraph; the least skilled cook help, peeling potatoes with power driven equipment has a higher labour productivity (real output) than a housewife using a kitchen knife.

Discussion of evaluations based on wages
for market equivalent qualifications

   Basic assumptions.   Evaluations based on wages paid for market jobs presenting profiles similar to the homemaker's (see 4.1.3) assume that, in the market itself, wage rates are related to job profiles, and that these relations are applicable to non-market activities. Although the first assumption is to a certain extent verified, as witnessed by the existence of nationwide sets of coefficients, it is also true that, in the labour market, economic circumstances, labour supply and demand, professional organisations' pressure, and a whole set of implicit industrial society values interact with the theoretical job evaluation frame and bear on it. As a result, a non-negligible amount of a posteriori pragmatic rationalisation is incorporated in what should not be mistaken for a purely rational and objective evaluation.

As for the second assumption, how would the household fit and fare in the nation-wide job-evaluation schemes, given the household's non-market, non-competitive characteristics, and its unpaid workers total lack of professional or pressure organizations? Job evaluation techniques were initially developed for scaling jobs within single enterprises, then extended to sector-wide and even nation-wide comparisons; they define relative positions within hierarchical systems. Is the household a hierarchical system per se, as an enterprise? Or to what hierarchical system do its unpaid workers relate to?

Job evaluation techniques emphasise "major duties" and usually define as "major" the activities consuming the larger proportion of work time. This point of view is, however, not shared by all. H. Schulz-Borck argues that, in the business world, a person employed as a manager is chosen according to the highest level task that he or she will be expected to do, and continues to be a manager even when doing simple routine tasks. (Schulz-Borck, 1975, p. 84). How would job evaluation "major" duties influence the rating of the homemaker's job? So defined, her "major" duties are routine tasks, while social values refer to the homemaker's "major" duties in the welfare of the family, the education of children, the management of resources, etc.

Limited substitution between market and non-market work (chapter 2) induces differentiated sex roles in the household and in employment, and imposes the routine tasks on those assigned to unpaid household work; how do such "constrained" routine tasks influence the rating of homemaker's job? Do they result in a low-grade job-rating, a situation likely to occur in societies where the supply of educated manpower is relatively small and skilled intellectual work relatively highly valued. Or do they correspond to the rating of jobs for which the labour supply tends to decrease as a result of more widespread education, a trend susceptible of inducing rising rewards for manual work? These are some of the questions remaining to be answered by further research in this approach.

The potential of job analysis techniques for obtaining a quantitative monetary evaluation of non-market activities is not clear yet: the attempts so far are limited in number; the professionals who have used them have expressed warnings about the interpretation of results which they consider as "a starting point for further research and investigation" (Arvey and Begalla, 1975, p. 517) or they have purposedly stopped at the job analysis itself and have not pursued the exercise in the wage imputation direction (Schulz-Borck, 1975 ; Bund Schweiz. Frauenorg. und Betriebswissensch. Inst. der ETH Zürich, 1981).

At present, the main contribution of this approach is qualitative: it describes work inputs in household production, from the angle of industrial psychology or of personnel management. While requiring choices that reflect the personal and social values of those performing the analysis, the approach permits qualitative comparisons with work inputs in the market sector.

22

Discussion of evaluations based on forgone wage
or opportunity cost of time

Basic assumptions. Evaluations based on forgone wage or opportunity cost of time are derived from the micro-economic theory of household behaviour (4.1.4). This theory rests on a number of explicit and implicit assumptions: rational behaviour of utility maximising well-informed individuals, having choices and choosing freely in a competitive market, reaching equilibrium conditions, etc. No attempt will be made here at summarising the ongoing debate for which reference is made to the specialised literature (see among others, the authors mentioned in 4.1.4). Comments formulated in the following paragraphs, are relative to the objectives of this study: assessment of the method based on opportunity cost of time, for the economic evaluation of unpaid work inputs in the household.

The fundamental tenet of this evaluation method is that the forgone wage that would correspond to time worked in the market, yields the value the household places on the unpaid work time of the member concerned, or its lower or upper limits according to circumstances (Kreps, 1971, p. 66; Gronau, 1973b, p. 168; Ferber and Birnbaum, 1980, p. 389).

Substitution of non-market work for market work. It should be noted that the theory is based on the marginal value of the last unit of market time which, in equilibrium, is assumed to be of equal value as the last unit of non-market time. This implies that market and non-market work can be substituted the one for the other in units, until equilibrium is reached. In practice this condition is rarely verified because of labour market and household functions constraints (chapter 2). Empirical research resorts to a simplification: the forgone wage yields the value of non-market time, full time or part-time, and the possibility to substitute globally the one for the other is taken for granted.

Substitution or addition? This method, deriving the value of non-market time from the value of market time, rests on the possibility of substituting the one for the other; it cannot therefore account for the unpaid household work the gainfully occupied performs in addition to market work, or for its counterpart by the non-employed. The fact that non-market work is often added to market work is disregarded although time-use studies show that this is a current situation. Is non-market work, which is performed in addition to employment, of higher value than the market wage and, therefore, not considered by the household for substitution? Or is it of lower value, but used as such because time is more plentiful than money? Is it of higher, lower or equal value as the "normal" hours (i.e. the counterpart of the eight hour day) of full-time homemakers? These questions, to our knowledge, are not tackled.

Determination of the reference wage. Some of the points being debated are relative to the choice of the reference wage. In the case of the gainfully employed, which is the wage to be considered for the imputation? The one corresponding to the main job, or to overtime (usually higher), or to moonlighting (possibly lower)? Which of these jobs compete in time allocation with household work? (Morgan, 1978, p. 207). What is the opportunity cost of time of a full-time homemaker with no record of gainful

23

employment? Average wages have been used to try and solve this last problem.

Part of household working time is constrained at intervals such that the remaining unconstrained time units may not be compatible with labour market employment conditions. What is the impact of such circumstances on the immediate opportunity cost of time? What is the opportunity cost of time of a person spending some years out of employment? Ferber and Birnbaum find these market factors play a major role in reducing the value of non-market work (in addition to men-women wage differentials discussed in 4.2.1), particularly when the evaluation is based on opportunity cost of time, but also with other wage-based evaluations. (Ferber and Birnbaum, 1980).

As pointed out in chapter 2, the market and non-market sectors appear related, as a certain amount of labour substitution can occur between the two; the relation between time values of market and non-market work is not a simple equality, not at a given moment of time nor over a life-span.

Distinct time markets. Because of limited substitution and because of constrained work capacity allocation, non-market and market time can to a certain extent be considered as belonging to two relatively distinct time markets (see discussion of labour productivity and value of time, in chapter 2). A larger fraction of non-market time will be used in productive activities, regardless of labour productivity level, if, because of monetary constraints, the household is anxious to forgo expenses. The reverse may also be true: at high-income levels, the emphasis may be placed on saving on household work time. In the first case, the value of household time measured in real output (at market prices of goods and services produced) may turn out to be lower than the market wage; in the second, it may turn out to be higher. There is no reason to assume that the value of household time should be equal to the market wage.

Real household output vs potential market output. One disturbing result of evaluations based on opportunity cost of time is that, for the same physical output (e.g. a load of washed dishes), the value is different if the person performing the activity is a law-school graduate or only went to school until age 14. The result is disturbing because the purpose is to evaluate unpaid work inputs in relation to their real output, and not in relation to their potential output in the market.

Another aspect of this paradox is the following. Consider two housewives, one with high and the other with low earning capacity. The second may tend to produce in the household certain goods and services which the first has stopped producing. The higher market wage of the first indeed sets at a higher value the equilibrium point; or, in other words, it "doesn't pay" for her to perform household tasks yielding a lower product than her market wage. Although the second housewife is producing a larger volume of real output, the value of her production will appear as lower because it is valued at opportunity cost of time.

Value or cost? The question may be raised whether the full-time housewife forgoes a market wage because her household work is valued as much or more than this wage, as postulated in the theory, or because the household can afford to forgo this income? In the latter perspective, the forgone wage appears rather as a *cost* of household production.

24

If the real value of household output of a full-time housewife is larger than the forgone wage, the household is operating "economically", it is making profit. If the real output has a lower value than the forgone wage, it is not operating "economically"; a situation which may call for several explanations: the household is not behaving rationally, or it has no choice because of local labour market conditions, or its overall money income is sufficiently high for subsidising household production for reasons other than economic (see above, remarks on household being able to function while ignoring its input/output flows), etc. Among women with the same wage-earning capacity, some may take up employment if their income from other sources is low, while others may choose to be full-time homemakers when other income is high. These different choices do not, however, mean that they attribute different values to household time, but only that the one can afford a choice the other cannot. It would, therefore, seem erroneous to equate the forgone wage with the *value* placed on household time; a range of other considerations may determine the choice.

Utility vs value in exchange. It might be argued that, particularly in recent research, what is being equated to the forgone wage is not "economic" value (value in exchange) but the overall utility or disutility of unpaid household work vs market work, including, for instance, satisfaction derived from work. Utility however falls outside the scope of the definition adopted in chapter 2: the activities being evaluated are those which can be delegated. If the scope of the evaluation goes beyond this definition, its results cannot be compared to the GNP which measures value in exchange, not utility. (The disutility of long journeys to and from work, or of repetitive dull work, does not change the value of the output accounted for in GNP.)

Macro-economic level. At the aggregate level, the use of opportunity cost of time as imputed wage for household work time raises another problem: it postulates that all persons concerned by the imputation, say housewives, have freely chosen to do so when exercising their choices. Situations in which there is no free choice (e.g. lack of employment opportunity, social mores, etc.) are disregarded, while their impact on opportunity cost of time may be large, possibly making it tend towards zero (Edwards, 1980, p. 12).

Net cost. Returning to the concept of cost, the forgone wage represents the value of what the same time input would have produced in the market. To obtain the net cost, to the economy, to the household, the real value of household output has to be deducted from the forgone wage; the resulting difference can be positive, negative or nil.

In this "cost" perspective, restricted to economic aspects, the theory might be reformulated in the following manner: the economically-minded housewife will shift to market work when the *net monetary income* generated by employment will be larger than the *real income forgone in household production,* so that total income (money plus real) will be larger than before employment. The claim is not made here that to be economically minded is the only alternative. Similar formulations could be presented for, say, the juridically minded housewife, who would shift to market work even if it is less productive than housework, in order to guarantee for herself firmer patrimonial rights in case of marriage dissolution. Or for the socially conscious housewife who, in the same economic circumstances, would turn to market work because it confers higher

25

social status.

Restricting the analysis to the immediate situation, without considering long-term effects of non-employment on opportunity cost of time, the net monetary income consists of a wage (W), minus job related additional expenses (AE) (taxes, transportation, additional clothing) and minus substitution expenses (SE) for goods and services not anymore produced in the household.

$$\text{net monetary income} = W - (AE + SE)$$

The real income forgone in household production is the difference between full household production (HP) when not employed, and reduced household production (hp) during employment when certain goods and services are no longer produced in the household and are substituted by goods and services purchased in the market.

$$\text{forgone real income} = HP - hp$$

The economically minded housewife will take up employment when

$$W - (AE + SE) \geq HP - hp$$

Conversely she will give up employment when

$$W - (AE + SE) \leq HP - hp$$

The net monetary income, $W - (AE + SE)$, corresponds to monetary transactions which can be measured; it expresses, in monetary terms, the limits of the difference $(HP - hp)$. It does not give the absolute value of either of the real incomes, HP or hp.

Micro-economic level. At the household level, the forgone wage is one of the elements of time allocation decisions. Such decisions, however, also require a perception of the value of non-market work, value which, as just discussed, is not provided by the opportunity cost of time method. The method assumes that the value of non-market work is known to the rational household which then tends towards the equilibrium point.

Discussion of evaluations based on average wages
of market workers and legal minimum wages

Household work evaluation methods based on average wages of market workers (4.1.5) share one major characteristic with methods based on forgone wage: they relate to the value of a potential market output, and not to the household real output. They, however, avoid the difficulties arising with opportunity cost of time for unpaid household workers of differing educational level.

Average wages are used, in particular, as a solution to the problem of the undetermined opportunity cost of time of full-time homemakers. Sometimes average female wages are used; sometimes average wages of all market workers are used, as a corrective for men/women wage differentials (4.2.1). Such averages, however, probably do not represent the average opportunity cost of time of full-time homemakers because of the impact of market factors (Ferber and Birnbaum, 1980).

The legal minimum wage was used for teenagers in an evaluation where wages for market equivalent functions were used for adults, the assumption being that teenagers' labour productivity is lower than that of adults. Again, the evaluation is related to a potential output in the market, not to real productivity in the household. In addition, market factors inducing lower wages for teenagers, affect the evaluation.

Discussion of evaluations based on wage
in kind i.e. non-cash benefits

We are aware of only one estimate where the housewife's "wage" is equated to non-cash benefits (Bergmann, 1980; see 4.1.6). The author derives from consumer expenditures, a measure of the decline in "standard of living" entailed by marriage or, in other words, the cost of taking a wife on board; we do not agree with this particular analysis of consumer expenditures and discuss it in some detail, in 5.2 below. Although this was not directly the purpose of Bergmann's evaluation, wages calculated on the market value of non-cash benefits could be considered for the evaluation of unpaid work inputs in the household. They could, in principle, afford an indication of the amount of money the wage-earner is willing to deduct from his monetary income in exchange for the utility derived from marriage, i.e. the price (cost) he is willing to pay for this utility.

Beyond this theoretical consideration, difficulties would however arise with this method of imputation, particularly at the aggregate level. Among these difficulties, those relating to the measurement of utility have already been discussed above. Another difficulty is that the method is strongly sensitive to overall household income, and bears a very weak relation, if any, to real product generated by unpaid household productive activity; for the same household product, the wage may be low or high.

Household production entails forgone expenses; accounted for at market prices, they may be larger, equal or smaller than the corresponding non-cash benefits. Only in the latter case may one speak of a cost. This situation is more likely to occur at high income levels with no children present; and even then, the housewife's unpaid activity may indirectly contribute to higher wages of the money earner, e.g. wifes of professionals entertaining for public relations purposes. As discussed in 5.2, monetary outlays for market goods are closely interwoven with forgone expenses resulting from non-monetary production. It is very difficult to disentangle what is a "cost" born because of marriage, from what is an increase in standard of living resulting from the wife's non-market activity, one component of marriage utility.

The evaluation of non-cash benefits as a wage in kind may, however, prove useful at the micro-economic level (e.g. property settlement in divorce cases) if the concept of *cost of a housewife* is abandoned, and replaced by the consideration that she shares benefits she contributed to create.

4.3 Conclusion on Wage-based Evaluation Methods

In this chapter, evaluation methods were reviewed which derive from market wages the imputed wage of unpaid work in the household. From this imputed wage, the value of household product is then estimated at the value of factor inputs, according to the national accounting convention for products not sold to the consumer.

For processes occurring outside the market price-fixing mechanisms, it is necessary to try and find, in the market, substitutes of which the price can be imputed on their non-market equivalent. One possibility is to find the price of substitute labour inputs. This is what the first wage-based estimates did when borrowing from the market the wages of substitute polyvalent household workers. Although this evaluation method now may present problems, its rationale at the moment it was introduced in the early 1920s, was in line with the goal pursued by the evaluation: the assessment at market prices, of that part of the national income which is not accounted for because it is produced and consumed in kind in the household without passing through the market.

The discussion of the other wage-based evaluation methods pointed at some common problems and at some particular problems raised by each method. Perhaps the major recurring problem, besides the selection of appropriate reference wages, is that the values arrived at are related to market productivity and not to household productivity: these values are sensitive to factors affecting market wages, but extraneous to the household; they bear no relation to the value of the output in kind generated by unpaid household work.

About the relative magnitude of what happens on both sides of the line separating the market and non-market sectors, wage-based evaluations don't tell anything more than the time-use data on which they rely. The volume of household time-inputs is the significant element in these evaluations; the market wages selected then act as coefficients reflecting the assumptions underlying their selection, and the labour market factors bearing on them.

The interactions between the two sectors i.e. the forces pulling or pushing labour and production from the one to the other, are, in principle, globally accounted for in the micro-economic theory of household behaviour. Analytically however their interaction is not apparent: evaluations based on opportunity cost of time reflect changes in the real value of market wages and not in households' real output, a situation also true of the other wage-based evaluations.

28

CHAPTER 5

Unpaid Work Evaluations based on the Market Value of Outputs

Household output resulting from unpaid work has been evaluated on the basis of the price of a market substitute, or on the basis of consumer expenditures for related inputs.

5.1 Output Value based on Price of Market Replacement

This approach imputes on non-market household output, the value (price) of equivalent market goods and services which could be used as replacement, global or specific, of the household product or which are similar to the household product. Overall care of infants, of the ill, of the aged in institutions are examples of global replacements; meals at a restaurant, shirts washed and ironed in commercial laundries, commercially prepared jams are examples of specific replacements or equivalents.

C. Clark was the first to base a value imputation on global replacement; his evaluation applied to the United Kingdom (Clark, 1958). Clark's method was applied to Belgium (Chaput-Auquier, 1959); courts use it in several countries (Clarke and Ogus, 1978). An estimate based on specific replacements was performed in the United States (Morgan, David, Cohen and Brazer, 1962), and on a market equivalent production in Finland (Suviranta and Mynttinen, 1981).

C. Clark bases his evaluation of the monetary value of household operation on the cost of keeping adults and children in institutions, deducting expenditures for housing, food and clothing. Institution and household operation are economically different: institutions can afford scale economies but incur administration costs, whereas neither exists in the household, where the emphasis is on personalised care. The value thus arrived at may well constitute a lower limit for household services. In addition, C. Clark attempts an intertemporal comparison which requires assumptions about the relative value of goods and services at successive stages of economic development, assumptions which seriously impair the values arrived at.

Morgan et al. estimate covering home-grown food, home additions and repairs, is based on the consumer-producer subjective evaluation of the money saved by doing things himself. Suviranta and Mynttinen based their monetary evaluation of housecleaning on the cost of an equivalent function performed for pay: the cost, per square meter, for cleaning day-care centers. Relating this cost (materials and equipment excluded) to dwellings' surface and to time devoted to housecleaning, they calculate an imputed wage for unpaid housecleaning. This is the only wage imputation based on output of which we are aware.

5.2 Output Value derived from related Consumer Expenditures

Evaluations based on consumer expenditures for inputs related to specific household outputs were made in the United States (Reid, 1947; Hirsch, 1959; Bergmann, 1981).

M. Reid's analysis of certain family expenditures in order to determine the volume of household production is discussed above in 3.1.2. E. Hirsch's estimate of the value added by "do-it-yourself" home activities, is based on the assumption that the income thus generated must be higher than the initial investment in equipment and raw materials, "as one of the purposes of do-it-yourself is to allow a saving" in money expenditure; the way the value added is estimated, is however not indicated.

B. Bergmann's evaluation was already discussed (4.1.5, 4.2.2), for its imputation of a wage in kind corresponding to non-cash benefits. The monetary value of this wage is calculated by means of an analysis of consumer expenditures which is questionable from the very point of view of household's real output. Bergmann derives the value of the benefits in kind, from consumer expenditures on clothing, taking them as an indicator of the standard of living. She finds that childless married men need twice the income of single men to afford the same clothing expenses. The difference between the two incomes is supposed to represent "the cost of a housewife to a childless married man". In fact what is obtained in this way is not "the cost of a housewife" but the forgone expenses of the married man as a result of the wife's household production. Typical of these forgone expenses are those related to care of clothing, to meals at home instead of meals taken out, etc. To assume, therefore, that expenditure on clothing can be used as an index of the comparative standard of living of a single man and of a child-free married man, is wrong; the latter can afford the same standards in clothing as the former, but with a lower outlay of money because of the housewife's unpaid laundering and ironing, and because of the lower wear and tear imposed on clothes by household technology.

Scale economies (housing, household operation) are afforded by the couple in addition to the above-mentioned forgone expenses, resulting in different overall patterns of money and time expenditures. As a result of pooling income-generating activities (cash and real income), the couple may end up with, for instance, better living quarters and/or better transportation facilities; with more or less leisure; etc. In addition, consumers' expenditures should not be considered separately from overall consumption ("real consumption", Kendé, 1978); goods and services resulting from household productive activity should be considered along with those purchased on the market, and along with the corresponding time-investments. (Ferber and Birnbaum, 1977; Vickery, 1978). To separate the "additional" money outlays entailed by marriage vs single living, therefore, does not appear correct. B. Bergmann's proposal to consider non-cash benefits as a return on work-inputs can be retained at the micro-economic level, but the value of this wage in kind needs to be more directly evaluated from the market value of the benefits themselves.

30

5.3 Conclusion

The estimates reviewed in this section are based on the value of the product generated by unpaid work in the household. Evaluations of output for special activities have not been performed for many activities, perhaps owing to difficulties in determining the volume and nature of the household product to be evaluated at market prices. Nor has Clark's global approach been repeated elsewhere, except for Belgium. An explanation might be that life in institutions cannot, quality wise, be considered a satisfactory replacement for life in a household. (A claim C. Clark indeed does not make, as he only tries to assess the economic value of household services). This difficulty is not more serious than those encountered in the more widely used evaluation methods discussed in chapter 4.

CHAPTER 6

Conclusions

The evaluations reviewed in the preceding chapters aim at assessing, at the household level or at the aggregate level, the economic importance of productive activities which, although similar in nature to market activities, are usually not included in national account statistics, while their market counterparts are.

6.1 Scope and Goals of the Study

The scope of this study is on the evaluation methodology of unpaid household work. We, therefore, have refrained from discussing extensively both what is to be measured and the existing evaluation results. M. Reid's operational definition of what is economic among household activities was adopted as a point of reference. It was noted that only two of the estimates reviewed deal with household non-market activities other than housewives' services in the home ;perhaps a result of tradition established in the early days of national accounting when housewives' services were considered the largest single item missing in the accounts. For a discussion of the values arrived at by different authors, reference was made to reviews by Hawrylyshyn (1976) and Murphy (1980).

Several goals were pursued in our study :

- to outline the variety of evaluation methods which have been applied to unpaid household work in industrialised economies ;

- to examine the economic foundations of these evaluation methods, particularly with respect to household economic circumstances ;

- to illustrate how each method contributes to assessing the relative magnitude of non-market production vs market production ;

- to determine whether these evaluation methods contribute to clarifying the mechanisms governing the interactions between the market and non-market sectors.

Covering a wide range of evaluation methods, we have tried to analyse in some depth the assumptions underlying them, their theoretical meaning and their effectiveness in achieving the goals for which they were initially designed or used. In order to perform our analysis, we distinguished between evaluation methods which express their results in what we called "volume" units, and those using monetary values; we further distinguished methods measuring inputs from those measuring ou:puts.

33

6.2 Evaluations based on Volumes of Inputs or of Outputs

Evaluations relating to the volume of inputs are expressed in number of workers involved, in number of hours or in quantities of goods consumed in the productive process. Evaluations relating to the volume of output are expressed in quantities of goods or services produced.

Volume based evaluations contribute to one of the goals pursued with non-market production evaluation: the determination, at the aggregate level, of its relative importance to market production. This goal is best achieved by evaluations expressed in number of workers or in time. They illustrate the work effort directed at satisfying human needs and wants, through market and non-market productive activity respectively. Evaluations expressed in other units (e.g. weights), while giving interesting indications on orders of magnitude for specific productive activities, do not lend themselves to all desirable levels of aggregation. It can thus be said that volume based evaluations contribute to the assessment of the relative magnitude of what happens on both sides of the line separating the market and non-market sectors. They, however, do not contribute to clarifying the mechanisms governing the interactions between the two sectors.

Volume based evaluation methods do not take into account market or household production circumstances and, therefore, are not influenced by them. All they assess is the input consumed (work, goods) or the output produced; the efficiency of the productive process, in the market or in the household, plays no role and, therefore, is not highlighted by these evaluation methods.

The validity of evaluations based on the volume of work inputs is strongly dependent on the quality of the corresponding evaluation of the number of workers involved in unpaid household work, or of the time consumed in household production. The latter is the object of current research on time-use but the accuracy of the data varies greatly between surveys.

6.3 Evaluations based on the Value of Work Inputs

Evaluations relating to the monetary value of unpaid household work (inputs) are based on the value of equivalent work in the market i.e. on market wages. Wages used as a basis for the imputation are those of substitute household workers, or of workers performing, in market enterprises, functions similar to those performed in the household or tasks requiring similar qualifications. Alternatively wages forgone in the market by unpaid household workers, or average wages, are taken as the basis of the imputation.

Evaluations based on wages of substitute household workers come closest to the goal pursued: the assessment at market prices of the relative magnitude of non-market production or, rather, of that part of it which can be delegated to others. But these evaluations come closest to this goal, only if their underlying assumptions are verified. These assumptions are that such substitute workers be actually available in the labour market, at the same hours of work, responsibility level, qualifications, etc. corresponding to unpaid household work, and that all elements of remuneration (not only wages, but also employment benefits, overtime rates, etc.) be accounted for. It was found that these conditions were more likely to obtain at earlier stages of

34

industrialisation than they are at present in the most advanced industrialised societies. It was suggested that one of the reasons for the spreading unavailability of substitute household workers might be that the household is, for certain economic functions, competing unfavourably with the market sector: the domestic wages it pays might be too low for the worker if compared to other wages offered in the market. At the same time, these domestic wages might be too high for the household if compared to the price of labour-saving equipment. If this hypothesis was verified, such wages could not be considered as setting a satisfactory standard for the evaluation of unpaid work.

All other wage-based evaluations suffer of a major drawback: the values arrived at are related to productivity in the market and not to productivity in the household; they are sensitive to factors affecting market wages but which are unrelated to household productivity; they carry no relation to the value of the output in kind generated by unpaid household work. Apart from these fundamental difficulties, wage-based evaluation methods face problems for the selection of appropriate reference wages in the market. They also are dependent on the accuracy of the time-use data they rely upon.

The discussion of evaluations based on forgone wage or opportunity cost of time induced us to question one of this method's fundamental assumptions: the possibility to substitute freely market work for non-market work at the margin; this possibility appears limited by labour market and household work constraints to such an extent that non-market and market work appear to belong to two relatively distinct time categories. Questions were also raised about unpaid household work which is not substituted by but is additional to market work, and which the method is unable to evaluate; about the choice between market and non-market work: is it determined by the assessment of a value, the value of unpaid household work, as postulated in this method, or is it primarily the result of a monetary constraint? At the macro-economic level, the appropriateness was questioned of comparing the household's imputed value which includes utility, to national income figures which do not include it. At the micro-economic level, even if all other assumptions about free substitution, etc. were satisfied, the net market wage could only indicate the upper or lower value of the real income forgone when substituting market work for non-market work; it does not yield the absolute value of the total real income generated in the household, before or after entering market work.

Wage-based evaluations offer the advantage of being relatively easy to handle at the aggregate level. In the present state of the art, the difficulties summarised above shed however doubts about their validity on theoretical grounds. A proposal is made in section 6.6, for further research to determine whether certain market wages constitute an approximation sufficiently close to the value of household output, for them to continue to be used in evaluations.

What is the contribution of wage-based evaluations as regards the clarification of the interactions between the market and non-market sectors? What do they tell us about the forces pulling or pushing labour and production from the one to the other? In principle these interactions are globally accounted for in the micro-economic theory of household behaviour, which is the theoretical frame of evaluations based on opportunity cost of time. Analytically, however, these interactions are not apparent; furthermore, evaluations based on opportunity cost of time fluctuate with the real value of market wages and not with households' real output. This situation is also true of the

35

other wage-based evaluations.

6.4 Evaluations based on the Value of Household Output

Evaluations based on the market value of household output are not numerous. Perhaps because it is difficult to determine the volume and nature of household product. Perhaps also because it is difficult to select, in the market, equivalent goods and services to be used as price reference. These evaluations meet the goal of illustrating the relative magnitude of non-market vs market production. They do not contribute to clarify the mechanisms governing the interactions between the two sectors.

6.5 General Comments

Some general comments need to be made about the evaluation of unpaid household work. They relate to the purpose of the evaluations, to the complementarity of evaluation methods and to the impact of social values on the economic evaluation.

Purpose of evaluation.   Some of the evaluations are purely academic; others are established with particular purposes in view: improvement of national income accounts, sometimes in order to facilitate intertemporal or interspatial comparisons, social policy (evaluation of total real income), guidance to households for resources allocation, property distribution in marriage dissolution, etc.

None of the evaluation methods under review gives per se an entirely satisfactory image of the economic importance of household productive activities. This is perhaps inevitable as values have to be imputed and are therefore artificial. It is important, therefore, that the assumptions underlying the various evaluation methods be explicit; they set limitations on the meaning of the evaluation which are to be considered when choosing and applying a method with a particular application in view. For instance, in economic policy formulation, the question may arise whether a transfer of production and of labour power from the household to the market sector would increase the overall, market and non-market, value of national income. To answer this question, the value of the income generated by unpaid work in the household, before and after the transfer, has to be estimated. An estimate based on the price of market substitutes of equivalent quality (wage of substitute household workers, price of substitute market good or services) might yield an acceptable approximation, *only if* such substitutes are, and will be, actually available at the all-inclusive cost retained for the evaluation. Only at this condition may the estimate be considered related to market values.

Intertemporal comparisons are difficult to achieve because of lack of longitudinal data and because of the weaknesses of the evaluation methods; only a few intertemporal comparisons have been attempted and their results are to be used with caution. Interspatial comparisons would require careful handling because of cultural differences; none is attempted in the evaluations covered in this study.

Complementarity of evaluation methods. Several evaluation methods can

36

usefully complement each other; this complementarity is perceived by those authors who use several methods for their estimates. For example, at the aggregate level, evaluations expressed in volumes such as number of workers or hours of work, yield an image of the work effort absorbed respectively in the market and non-market sectors. They do not indicate the economic contribution of these respective work efforts (how successful they are, how much they contribute) towards the satisfaction of human needs and wants. Part of these contributions, the part of which the performance can be delegated to others, can be assessed by evaluations expressed in monetary value. The two approaches, volume and value, are complementary.

Another instance of complementarity can be found at the micro-economic level: property division and alimony in marriage dissolution. Property, alimony, wages are expressed in money; the trend is therefore to resort to evaluations also expressed in monetary units (value) to achieve comparable figures assessing the unpaid services contributed by the housewife. Wages of substitute household workers, opportunity cost of time, wage in kind qualify in a complementary manner for this evaluation. Marriage can, however, be viewed as a contract whereby partners pool their work potential under social constraints, regardless of the economic productivity of the tasks each is assigned; the amount of effort, of work time, may then provide a further complementary measure for the determination of each partner's share. Again volume and value based estimates appear complementary.

Social values. As evaluation methods were reviewed, attention was drawn in the course of the study, to the impact of social values on the economic evaluation. Such an impact is particularly evident in the selection of market reference wages, or in the definition of qualifications, responsibilities and major duties pertaining to household work. In other cases, social factors are more deeply interwoven and their impact on the economic evaluation is not immediately apparent. One instance is afforded by the division of labour according to sex, which, usually, assigns major responsibility to women for household production. This primary social role has an impact on women's earning capacity in the market, i.e. results in their wages being lower than men's on the average. When women's wages are imputed on unpaid household work, the bias imposed by social roles on the market wage they can command, is reflected on the imputed household wage. In other words, women's economic contribution in the market is underrated because their "primary" role is in the household; but their economic contribution in that very household is underevaluated because their role in the market is considered to be only secondary.

Such interrelations between economic and social factors are part of social reality; the search for a "purely economic" evaluation would end up, if it were at all feasible, in an abstract concept disconnected from the society to which it is supposed to pertain. As mentioned already above for the economic assumptions underlying the various evaluation methods, it is important that an effort be made to make explicit the social factors having an impact on the evaluation.

6.6 Perspectives for further Research

At the end of the discussion of several methods used for the evaluation of unpaid work in the household, what are the lines this review suggests for further research?

Evaluations based on the volume of work inputs. Expressed in number of workers or of work hours, they provide important information and should be pursued. They illustrate the work effort in non-market production, thus permitting comparisons, at the micro-economic and at the aggregate levels, with the work effort in market production. Such comparisons have, so far, only aimed at defining gross orders of magnitude. More refined comparisons between the market and non-market sectors will become possible as more precise data become available on use of time: at home, at work in the formal and informal sectors, for transportation to work, for work related education and training, etc. Such time-use data are being collected; data collection methodologies are being improved by researchers specialised in the field. Reliable time-use data at more than one point in time, when available, will permit intertemporal comparisons. Time-use data collected for household work evaluation purposes is usually supplemented with the collection of information relative to the presumed volume of output: number of household members, number and age of children, employment status of wife, etc. Such output parameters, or possibly more refined assessments of output if they can be established, should further be combined with information on household monetary income and on household members educational level. Such data would be useful for extrapolations at the aggregate level when sufficient time-use data will be available to permit the extrapolation.

Evaluations based on the volume of inputs other than work and of household outputs. Expressed in activity-specific quantities of goods or services they are rare and are likely to remain so. They do not lend themselves to aggregation or to comparison with measurements of other economic activities.

Evaluations based on the value of work inputs, i.e. wage-based evaluations. Because they are expressed in monetary units, they are, on the contrary, very convenient to use and were, indeed, adopted by two thirds of the authors quoted in this review. In principle, the results of these evaluations, illustrate the value of unpaid work inputs in the household; they have, however, been stretched to represent an evaluation of household output. We have questioned this connection between the value of household input and the value of household output, by stressing that household productive activities are determined by more than economic considerations, and that, in certain circumstances, from a strictly economic point of view, the household may be operating at a loss. With the exception of imputations based on wages of household substitute workers, we even questioned the imputation of market wages for household unpaid work. Our reticence is based on the fact that labour productivity may differ in the market and in the household. It seems to us, therefore, that further research in this area should be pursued in order to determine whether input and output values are related in the same manner in the market and in the household. This relationship could be explored at the *micro-economic level*. First by deriving imputed household wages for specific activities from the market values of household outputs (the price of corresponding market goods and services) divided by the related work time inputs. Then, by comparing these output-related imputed wages to the market wages of specialised substitute household workers, or of workers with similar functions or qualifications in market enterprises, or to average or forgone wages. These comparisons should reveal whether market wages are appropriate to use for unpaid household work evaluation; in the affirmative, the comparisons would indicate which wages are the most appropriate; if not, new modes of evaluation would have to be looked for. In addition, the comparison of imputed household wages for specific activities derived from the value of household output might reveal differences in labour productivity between the household and the market, and, thereby, provide an indication on the underlying influences causing activities to be performed in the market or non-market sectors.

Evaluations based on the value of household output. Expressed in monetary units, they are only few, in spite of the relative ease of establishing them at the macro-economic level. We were not able to explain the lack of interest in this evaluation method, as the difficulties it raises did not appear more serious than those raised by more "popular" methods. We, therefore, consider it worthwhile to pursue aggregate level evaluations based on the market value of output, and to search for satisfactory market equivalents which, together with their price, would yield the imputed value. These macro-economic evaluations might, in turn, be converted into imputed wages, by taking into account work time inputs. They would not necessarily yield the same values as the micro-economic evaluations proposed in the preceding paragraph, since they are the result of a global more comprehensive evaluation, and since they incorporate market wages in the imputation. The macro-economic evaluation also differs from the micro-economic one, in that it does not have the same analytical purpose, but aims at an aggregate estimate of unpaid household work.

Sociological research. Our review has indicated areas in which further sociological research may also contribute towards the evaluation of unpaid household work. The contribution of sociology to time-use research was already mentioned earlier in this section. Further thinking is required about the distinction between work and leisure or, perhaps more fundamentally, about what is to be considered work. The perception individuals have of the value, economic and other, of their own non-market activity, can be investigated by means of surveys as well as by job evaluation techniques, an exercise, as noted in our study, valid per se even if not pursued into a wage-based evaluation. And, perhaps most important, social research has to explicitly recognise how social values permeate economic thought.

6.7 Concluding Remarks

At the end of this study, after analysing different methodologies, it appears that further research is still required before the appropriateness of certain evaluation methods can be established on theoretical grounds. Given the state of the art, no single evaluation method answers the needs of all evaluation purposes. Nor can any simple rule be offered for field workers concerned with the evaluation of unpaid household work. It is possible, however, once the purpose of the evaluation has been defined, to devise a combination of methods for approximating, at least in order of magnitude, the relative value of unpaid household work compared to market work.

39

It is our personal conviction that, in spite of the very real difficulties encountered, the economic and socio-economic evaluation of unpaid household work is important. Too little is known about the relationships between the market sector and the household sector, and about their impact on one another. An economic sector, the household, consuming approximately one-half of the work effort even in industrialised societies, deserves more attention and research than it has been given until now. If meaningful decisions are to be taken in the economic, social and manpower fields, the economic and social value of unpaid household work has to be taken into account.

Summaries of Unpaid Work Evaluations

The evaluation summaries appear, in this appendix, in *chronological order*, by year; within a same year, they are arranged in alphabethical order.

They are preceded by a synoptic table permitting *access by author*.

Each evaluation summary includes:

a shortened bibliographical reference (full references are given in the bibliography);

country and period covered by the estimate;

level at which the evaluation is performed (micro or macro economic);

purpose of the evaluation;

evaluation method(s) used;

comments pertinent to the particular evaluation (general methodological discussions appear in chapters 3 to 5);

selected evaluation results given, in brackets, only as an indication of the orders of magnitude at stake in household production; as the object of this report is methodology, the values arrived at are not discussed and should not be used for comparisons (see chapter 2).

The authors' own wording is given, as much as possible, in quotation marks.

The evaluations are summarised according to the focus of the present study: for full analysis, readers are referred to the original publication.

Abbreviations

referring to evaluation methods :

CE	value of output, based on related consumer expenditures
I.a	volume of inputs other than work
I.t	volume of work inputs, in time
I.w	volume of work inputs, in workers
O.a	volume of output, by activity
P.MR	value of output, at price of market replacement
W.A	average wages
W.A.f	average wages of females
W.LM	minimum legal wage
W.MEF	wage, market equivalent function
[W.] MEQ	[wage,] market equivalent qualifications
W.NCB	wage in kind or non-cash benefits
W.OCT	forgone wage or opportunity cost of time
W.S	wage, substitute household worker
W.S.p	wage, substitute household worker, polyvalent
W.S.s	wage, substitute household worker, specialised

referring to economic level :

M	macro-economic level
m	micro-economic or household level

42

Synoptic Presentation of Evaluations

Authors	Date of publication	Country	Evaluation methods	Economic level
Adler and Hawrylyshyn	1978	Canada	W.MEF W.S.p W.A	M M M
Adret	1977	France	I.t	M
Andrews	1935	United States	W.S.p W.S.s	m+M m
Arvey and Begalla	1975	United States	W.MEQ	m
Bergmann	1981	United States	W.NCB + CE	m
Brody	1975	United States	W.MEF W.A.f W.S.p	m m m
Bund Schweiz. Frauen-org. und Betriebswiss. Inst. ETH, Zürich	1981	Switzerland	[W]MEQ	m
Cannon	1928	United States	W.S.p	m
Chaput-Auquier	1959	Belgium	W.S.p P.MR	M M
Chase Manhattan Bank	1972	United States	W.MEF	m
Clark	1958	United Kingdom	P.MR	M
Clarke and Ogus	1978	United Kingdom, Australia, France, Germany (Fed. Republic), New Zealand, United States	W.S.s W.OCT P.MR	m m m]
Danmark, Stat. Dept.	1948	Denmark	W.S.p	M
Danmark, Stat. Dept.	1951	Denmark	W.S.p	M

Authors	Date of publication	Country	Evaluation methods	Economic level
Dayre	1955	France	I.t	M
Deist-Bohner	1977	Germany (Fed. Republic)	[W]MEQ	m
Eisner	1978	United States	W.S.p	M
			W.S.s	M
Ferber and Birnbaum	1980	United States	W.OCT	m
			W.s.p	m
Fourastié	1965	France	I.t	M
Fürst	1956	Germany (Fed. Republic)	I.t	M
			W.S.p	M
			W.A.f	M
			O.a	M
Gage	1960	United States	W.S.s + (I.t + O.a)	m
Galbraith	1973	---	---	–
Gauger and Walker	1980	United States	W.MEF +	m +
			W.LM	M
Goldschmidt-Clermont	1952	United States	I.t	M
Gronau	1973a	United States	W.OCT	m
Gronau	1973b	Israel	W.A.f + W.OCT	m
Gronau	1976	United States	W.OCT	m
Gronau	1980	United States	W.OCT	m
Hauserman and Fethke	1978	United States	W.S.s + W.MEF + W.OCT	m
Hegeland	1975	Sweden	I.t	M

Authors	Date of publication	Country	Evaluation methods	Economic level
Hirsch	1959	United States	CE	M
Honkanen	1967	Finland	W.MEF	M
Japan, Economic Council	1973	Japan	W.A.f	M
Japan, Supreme Court	1975	Japan	W.A.f	m
Kendé	1978	France	W.S.s + W.MEF	m
Kendrick	1975	see Ruggles	1975	
Kendrick	1977	United States	W.S.s? W.MEF?	M
Kneeland	1929	United States	W.S.s I.w	m M
Kredietbank	1975	Belgium	W.A.f	M
Kreps	1971	United States	W.OCT	M
Kuznets	1941	United States	W.S.p	M
Kyrk	1953	United States	I.w	M
Lacasse	1971	Canada	W.S.s W.A.f	M M
Lindahl, Dahlgren and Kock	1937	Sweden	W.S.p	M
Lindberg	1943	Finland	W.S.p	M
Lindgren	1974	Finland	W.S.p	M
Machlup	1962	United States	W.A.f	M
Manning	1968	United States	I.t + O.a	m
Matolcsy and Varga	1938	Hungary	I.w W.S.p	M M

Authors	Date of publication	Country	Evaluation methods	Economic level
Mitchell, King, MacAulay and Knauth	1921	United States	W.S	M
Morgan, David, Cohen and Brazer	1962	United States	P.MR	m
Morgan, Sirageldin and Baerwaldt	1966	United States	I.t W.A	m m
Murphy	1978	United States	W.MEF W.A + W.A.f	M M
Nederlandse Gezinsraad	1972	Netherlands	W.MEQ + W.S. + W.OCT	m
Nordhaus and Tobin	1972	United States	W.A.f	M
Norge	1948	Norway	W.S.p	M
Proulx	1978	Canada	W.MEF	m
Pyun	1969	United States	W.OCT + W.S.s	m
Reid	1947	United States	I.w W.S.p CE I.a	M M m m
Rosen	1974	United States	W.S.p	m
Ruggles and Ruggles	1975	United States	W.S.s? W.MEF?	M
Schacht	1979	Germany (Fed. Republic)	W.MEF	m
Schulz-Borck	1975	Germany (Fed. Republic)	W.MEQ I.t	m M
Scott	1972	---	---	–

Authors	Date of publication	Country	Evaluation methods	Economic level
Shamseddine	1968	United States	W.S.s	M
Sirageldin	1969	United States	W.S.s + W.MEF W.OCT	m m
Stübler et al.	1967	Germany (Fed. Republic)	[W]MEQ	m
Suviranta and Heinonen	1980	Finland	O.a + I.t + W.MEF	M
Suviranta and Mynttinen	1981	Finland	O.a + P.MR	M
Walker	1955	United States	I.t + O.a	m
Walker and Gauger	1973	See update : Gauger and Walker, 1980		
Walker and Woods	1976	United States	I.t + O.a	m
Warren	1938	United States	I.t + O.a	m
Weinrobe	1974	United States	W.A.f	M
Weisbrod	1961	United States	W.S.p (+ O.a)	M
Wiegand	1953	United States	I.t + O.a	m

MITCHELL, KING, MACAULAY and KNAUTH . 1921

Income in the United States ; its amount and distribution, 1909–1919

United States   1909–1919

Macro-economic level

Purpose

To "indicate order of magnitude of housewives' contribution to national income ... a conjectural estimate of its money value" (p. 59).

Method
Wage, substitute household worker

Number of full-time housewives

multiplied by

"average pay of persons engaged in Domestic and Personal Service, a group that includes many other occupations besides female-domestics" (p. 59).

Comment

"Following common practice, we do not count as part of the national income anything for which a price is commonly not paid [with the exception of agricultural produce consumed by the families that produce it, and of the rental value of homes occupied by their owners (p. 42)]. On this score, we omit several of the most important factors in social well-being, above all the services of housewives to their families. Two awkward results follow from the exclusion: comparisons are thrown askew between communities ... which differ widely in the proportion of women who work at home and women who work for wages (as pointed out by Sir Josiah Stamp, 1919) ... Figures we get for the national income in successive years tend to exaggerate the increase in economic welfare" (pp. 57-58).

(Evaluation)

(Housework value ranges between 25 and 31 per cent of reported national income.)

CANNON . 1928

**The family finances of 195 farm families in Tompkins
County, New York, 1927-1928**
(Quoted in Reid, 1934 . pp. 168-9)

United States   1927-1928

Micro-economic level

Purpose

"Farm homemakers asked to estimate a rate of pay for their own work".

Method
Wage, substitute household worker, polyvalent

195 interviewed farm homemakers from Tompkins County, New York ..." in many cas
resorted to the rate of pay for women who had been hired to do housework ... value of the boar
furnished was then added ... no recognition was given to the managerial skill of the housewife,
to differences in skill, ... in extra effort ...".

(Evaluation)

(Average value of housework : US $ 1,044 per year.)

KNEELAND . 1929

Woman's economic contribution in the home
Annals American Academy of Political and Social Sciences

United States   1929 and 1920

Micro-economic and macro-economic levels

Purpose
To establish "a rough and hazardous guess of imputed earnings ... a lower and upper limit ..."
(p. 36).

Methods
a.   Micro-Economic level   *Wage, substitute household worker, specialised*
Time devoted to different tasks (time-use observations of two case studies)

multiplied by

"an amount slightly larger than houseworker's wage, for routine tasks, to compensate for lower efficiency, more wear and tear, etc. of hired help; two to three times as large for management, depending on personal efficiency; for other tasks, intermediate values based on wage rates customarily paid for each of these types of workers" (pp. 36-38).

Comment
"Arbitrary" (p. 35) judgement as to the respective value to be imputed to the various activities, because "it is practically impossible to employ a corps of specialised workers in the home" (p. 38). Income in kind of hired help is mentioned but not accounted for.

(Evaluation)
(Housework evaluated at ∼ US $ 3.000 per year.)

b.   Macro-Economic level   *Volume of work inputs, in workers*
number of full-time housewives

compared to

number of gainfully employed.

(Evaluation)

(21 million housewives; 42 million gainfully employed; housewives constitute one third of the working population.)

ANDREWS . 1935

Economics of the household ; its administration and finance

United States   1932

Micro-economic and macro-economic levels

Purpose

"To measure the money value of household [unpaid] labor income ... to estimate its lower limits" (p. 74).

Methods

a.   Micro-Economic Level   *Wage, substitute household worker, polyvalent*

Substituting unpaid "household labor ... by hired service of equal skill; ... lower limit: houseworker wage (US $ 50/month), fairer comparison : housekeeper wage (US $ 75/month) ; room and board (US $ 50/month) ; ... rural districts : at least half of this" ... (p. 74).

(Evaluation)

"A full-time housewife adds US $ 1,200 to 1,500 per year, to family income, not counting her full-management contribution and her managerial aid in the husband's outside occupation (farming, profession)" (p. 75).

b.   Micro-Economic Level   *Wage, substitute household worker, specialised*

"Time devoted by housewife to cooking, child care, laundry, etc."

multiplied by

"cost of substituting with specialised workers"

Comment

" ...Gives a larger money value [than *a.*] ... not inflated where she has real skill ... a complete substitution is not possible ... therefore total value of housewife's work exceeds these estimates based on the parts of her work which can be measured in money..." (p. 74).

(Evaluation)

(Calculation not performed.)

c. Macro-Economic Level   *Wage, substitute household worker, polyvalent*

Number of full-time homemakers

multiplied by

average housekeepers' pay, room and board not accounted for

(Evaluation)

("Unpaid household work amounted to 60 per cent of total monetary income of 1932, a depression year; to 28 per cent of 1929 income") p. 74.

LINDAHL, DAHLGREN and KOCK . 1937

**National income of Sweden,
1861–1930**

Sweden   1861-1930

Macro-economic level

Purpose

To establish an "approximate ... arbitrary ... estimate of the large item of domestic services rendered by wives and daughters ... for inclusion in national income estimates" (pp. 10, 214, 517).

Method

Wage, substitute household worker, polyvalent

"number of women, aged 15 or more, living at home i.e. not employed, plus half of the time of those working in agriculture (pp. 213 and 531),

multiplied by

"estimated average annual wages of domestic servants" (p. 532).

Comment

"...It is probable that the calculations which are only rough approximations ... understate the value of unpaid domestic services in the earlier part of the period..." (p. 239).

(Evaluation)

(In 1930, the value of unpaid domestic work was equivalent to 20 per cent of the national income inclusive of unpaid domestic services, and to 25 per cent of the national income exclusive of unpaid domestic services.

In 1861, 17.6 per cent of domestic work was performed by domestic servants; in 1930, 8.1 per cent.)

MATOLCSY and VARGA . 1938

**The national income of Hungary,
1924-1925 and 1936-1937**

Hungary   1924-1936

Macro-economic level

Purpose

To estimate the value of domestic work for inclusion in national income estimates.

Methods

a. *Volume of work inputs, in workers*

a.1   Number of households (assumed to be equal to number of houses and flats)

multiplied by

half a day of domestic work (assumed to be the amount of work required per housing unit)

(Evaluation: 354 million working days/year.)

a.2   Number of married women without other employment multiplied by half a day of domestic work plus number of married women with employment multiplied by a quarter of a day of domestic work

plus

number of domestic servants multiplied by a day of work.

(Evaluation: 357 million working days/year.)

Comment

The amount of time assumed by Matolcsy and Varga as necessary for household production, appears unrealistically low if compared to data yielded by time use studies.

(Evaluation *a.1* and *a.2*)

(Domestic work consumes 9 to 12.5 per cent of total national work effort.)

(continued overleaf)

---

b. *Wage, substitute household worker, polyvalent*

Number of working days as obtained in *a.* ₁ and *a.* ₂ above

multiplied by

"wages and keep of domestic servants in towns, and half of the current wage of female day-labourers in country households" or by a rough equivalent i.e. "66 per cent of current wage of female day labourers in agriculture" (p. 34).

(Evaluation)

(The value of domestic work is equivalent to 5.9 to 12.1 per cent of the total national income. "This nominal value fluctuates to a marked degree owing to variations in the current rates paid to day-labourers" (p. 66).)

WARREN , 1938 and 1940

Use of time in relation to home management

United States   1935

Micro-economic level

Purpose

Attempt to measure household production in terms of quantity of goods and services produced per unit of time. ("Work units" adapted from an agricultural productivity measure which scaled amounts of widely different kinds of work output, into units of time.)

Method
Volume of work inputs, in time, and *Volume of output, by activity*

In a survey of New-York State farm households, measures the average quantity of output for a specific task (e.g. number of items ironed, with a weighting for size and complexity of item), in a given time unit, under certain household conditions. The latter are defined by the one factor (task specific variable) that seems to be more closely related than others to the time spent (e.g. number of family members, or age of youngest child, or size of dwelling unit, etc.). For some household activities, this factor could not be identified, and no work unit could be computed.

KUZNETS . 1941

**National income and its composition,
1919-1938**

United States   1929

Macro-economic level

Purpose

To "approximate order of magnitude of household activities 'within the domestic circle and compare them with the activities whose end products are covered in our national income estimates" (p. 432) ... "a crude estimate" (p. 433).

Method
Wage, substitute household worker, polyvalent

Number of full-time housewives ("leaving out contributions of other household members not gainfully occupied — one for every five full-time housewives — and contributions of gainfully occupied persons, employed or not employd ; correction for domestic servants : negligible")

multiplied by

"average pay of domestic servants (US $ 900) in non-farm families, and of farm workers (US $ 600) in farm families" (p. 432-433).

Comment

"National income, as we compute it, is essentially an appraisal of the final net product of the business and public economies of the country, two of the three important social institutions that contribute to the production of economic goods ; it excludes completely the product of the third, the family .. This exclusion, characteristic of virtually all national income estimates, seriously limits their validity as measure of all scarce and disposable goods produced by the nation" (p. 10).

(Evaluation)

(Full-time housewives' services amounted in 1929 United States, to somewhat more than 25 per cent of the reported national income.)

LINDBERG . 1943

Suomen kansantulo vuosina 1926-1938
Suomen pankin suhdanne tutkimusosaston julkaisuja

Finland   1926-1938

Macro-economic level

Purpose
To estimate household work for comparison with national income estimates.

Method
Wage, substitute household worker, polyvalent

Number of families (on the assumption each family has one person, on average, performing housework exclusively)

multiplied by

average salary of domestic servants.

(Evaluation)

(Household work value amounts to 20 to 25 per cent of national income.)

REID . 1947

The economic contribution of homemakers
Annals American Academic of Political and Social Sciences

United States   1940-1945

Macro-economic and micro-economic levels.

1. **Purpose**   (macro economic level)

Assessment of the economic contribution of homemakers in relation to national income.

Methods

a.   Macro-Economic Level   *Wage of work inputs, in workers*

Number of full-time homemakers ("only those not gainfully employed even though those in the labor force ... have household responsibility", p. 63),

compared to

a. 1   number of able-bodied women and to number in the labour force

   (Evaluation: 1940 : 69 per cent of able-bodied women are homemakers ; 31 per cent are in the labour force.)

a. 2   number, male and female, in the labour force

   (Evaluation : 1940 : 55 full-time homemakers for every 100 persons in the labour force.)
   (p. 63)

b.   Macro-Economic Level   *Wage, substitute household worker, polyvalent*

Number of full-time homemakers

multiplied by

average earnings of domestic workers in non-farm homes, and of farm workers in farm homes. ("This wage basis can hardly be said to lead to an overstatement" (p. 65). Wages in kind not accounted for.)

(**Evaluation**: Value of household work is equivalent, in 1940, to 20 per cent and, in 1954, to 22 per cent of reported national income.)

2. Purpose   (micro-economic level)

Assessment of volume and nature of household production according to household's money income and to urban, rural non-farm and rural farm residence.

Methods

c.   Micro-Economic Level   *Value of output, based on related consumer expenditures*

Percentage of total food expenditure used for eating outside home

d.   Micro-Economic Level   *Volume of inputs other than work*

Percentage of flour incorporated in baked goods purchased, to flour for home baking. Same for laundry, sewing, etc.

(Evaluation)

("Farm families carry on more household production because of fewer opportunities to get commercial goods and services ... how income forces many families to do certain household tasks themselves ... The average money income ... per person ... (with corrections for food and housing costs) ... is lower in farm than in urban families") (p. 66).

"In cities, smoke and dust have increased the time needed for cleaning, ... the time and energy necessary per child (play supervision, special arrangements for experiences that formerly were part of household routine ...)" (p. 62).

3. Comment on micro-economic and macro-economic evaluations

Reid's micro-economic analysis (*c.* and *d.*) shows a larger *volume* of household production in farm families. The macro-economic evaluation (*b.*), however, understates its *monetary value* because of the imputation of lower wages on household work in farm homes. This discrepancy points at one of the difficulties raised by wage imputations which bear no relation to the volume of production.

DANMARK, STATISTISKE DEPARTEMENT . 1948

Nationalproduktet og nationalindkomsten 1930-1946
Statistiske Meddelelser

Denmark   1930-1946

Macro-economic level

Purpose

To estimate the value of the personal services provided at home, for comparison with net national product estimates.

Method
Wage, substitute household worker, polyvalent

Number of wives, grown-up daughters not occupied outside the family and widows head of family

multiplied by

average earnings of housekeepers.

(Evaluation)

(Unpaid household services amounted, in 1930, to 84 per cent and, in 1939, to 85,9 per cent of paid plus unpaid household services. Unpaid household services amounted in 1930, to 15 per cent and, in 1939, to 14.1 per cent of the net national product inclusive of unpaid household services.)

NORGE . 1948

Nasjonalinntekten i Norge, 1935-1943

Norge   1946-1948

Macro-economic level

Purpose

Inclusion of housewives' work in the first official figures of national income and expenditures for the years 1946 to 1948.

Method
Wage, substitute household worker, polyvalent

Number of housewives

multiplied by

wages (money and real income) of domestic servants.

DANMARK, STATISTISKE DEPARTEMENT . 1951

Nationalproduktet og nationalindkomsten 1946-1949
Statistiske Meddelelser

Denmark   1946-1949

Macro-economic level

Purpose
Evaluation of unpaid household services for inclusion in national income estimates.

Method
Wage, substitute household worker, polyvalent

Number of housewives and other adults (daughters) remaining at home

multiplied by

wages of domestic workers.

(Evaluation)

(Approximately DKR 200 million, for a GNP of DKR 399 million.)

GOLDSCHMIDT-CLERMONT . 1952

L'importance économique du travail domestique et ses liens
avec l'économie nationale américaine
Revue de l'Institut de Sociologie

United States   1940

Macro-economic level

Purpose

A crude assessment of household production in relation to overall American economic
activity.

Method
Volume of work inputs, in time

Number of hours worked in the market sector

compared to

number of hours worked in households (weekly average from U.S. Department of Agriculture,
Bureau of Home Economics, 1931)

multiplied by

number of households.

(Evaluation)

($\sim$ 105,000 million hours worked in the market sector; $\sim$ 130,000 million hours worked in
households.)

KYRK . 1953

The family in the American economy

United States   1950

Macro-economic level

Purpose

To determine order of magnitude of "productive effort devoted to consumer production" (p. 243).

Method

Volume of work inputs, in workers

"Number of persons able to work, aged 18 to 65, devoting their time to housework in their own homes"

compared to

"total population able to work, of the same age" (p. 243).

Comment

To be added : "others in school or gainfully employed" (p. 243).

(Evaluation)

(No other occupation than housework in own home : 32 per cent of total population able to work, aged 18 to 65.)

WIEGAND . 1953 and 1954

Use of time by full-time and part-time homemakers in relation to home management

---

United States   1950

Micro-economic level

Purpose

To pursue Warren's determination of "work units" (see : 1938, Warren).

Methods

Volume of work inputs, in time and *Volume of output, by activity*

Survey "study of time used for household activities by 250 full-time and part-time homemakers in upstate New York urban and farm households" (p. 6).

DAYRE . 1955

Habitat, services résidentiels et niveau de vie
Etudes et documents CRES
(Quoted in : Sullerot, 1965, pp. 107-108)

France   1955

Macro-economic level

Purpose

"To calculate, in hours, the global workload of the French nation".

Method
Volume of work inputs, in time

(Evaluation)

(Gainful employment, all categories	: 43,000 million hours
Unpaid household work	: 45,000 million hours
Studying time	: 12,000 million hours
Transportation to work	: 5,000 million hours.)

WALKER . 1955 and 1958

Homemaking work units for New York State households

United States   (~ 1950)

Micro-economic level

Purpose

Development of a measure of household production ... based on the concept of "work units" (see : 1938, Warren).

Method

Volume of work inputs, in time and *Volume of output, by activity*

Reanalysis of Wiegand's data (see : 1953, Wiegand) to isolate the specific variables exerting the greatest influence on the amount of time spent on six household tasks accounting for four fifths of housework time, and computation of the average times.

(Evaluation)

(Determinant variables : for meal preparation, complexity of meals served ; for regular house care, presence or absence of children ; for dishwashing, number of persons in household ; for care of family members, number and age of children ; etc.)

(Work units expressed in average hours per day ; e.g. work unit for washing dishes : two persons : 0.9 unit/day ; three persons : 1.0 unit/day ; work unit for care of family members : youngest member under two years : 2.0 units/day ; youngest member two to five years : 1.0 unit/day ; etc.)

FUERST . 1956

**Einkommen, Nachfrage, Produktion und Konsum des privaten
Haushaltes in der Volkswirtschaft**

Federal Republic of Germany   1953-1954

Macro-economic level

Purpose

"To determine in order of magnitude how productive contributions of the household compare with market contributions".

Methods

a. Volume of work inputs, in time

From time-use data in four persons households in which wife is not employed, derives average number of housework hours required per person ($\sim$ two hours/day); multiplies this figure by total population not in institutions, and compares to industry.

(Evaluation)

(32,400 million hours in housework; 11,000 million hours in industry i.e. in only one particular sector of market activity.)

b. Wage, substitute household worker, polyvalent

Number of housework hours (see *a*)

multiplied by

housekeeper hourly wage (1 DM).

Comment

"A minimal evaluation because it does not account for the "entrepreneurial" aspect of housewives' work (e.g. choosing combinations of production factors among several possibilities" (pp. 87 and 24).

(Evaluation)

(Housework value estimated to be DM. 32,400 million.)

c. *Average wages of females*

Number of housework hours (see *a*)

multiplied by

average female wages, in industry and other market sectors.

(Evaluation)

(Household work: DM. 34,600 to 42,000 million, to be compared to: industry, without construction (DM. 47,800 million), agriculture and forestry (DM. 11,800 million), total national income (DM. 107,000 million); i.e. household work amounts to 32 to 39 per cent of national income.)

Comments on *a, b* and *c*

These evaluations are "based on hours of work for lack of data permitting other approaches, e.g. market price of finished product (piecework approach instead of hourly wage). Amortisation of equipment e.g. service provided by stove, etc., should also be accounted for" (pp. 21-24 and 83).

d. *Volume of output, by activity*

Amount of transportation service provided by housewives in relation to food preparation: from average weight of food purchased by four-person households in one month (Statistisches Jahrbuch, 1954, p. 515) derives average of 1 kg per day per person in the household.

(Evaluation)

(Households transported in 1954 $\sim$ 16.200.000 tons of food equivalent to the weight of petrol transported by the Federal railways. (p. 58).)

CLARK . 1958

The economics of house-work
Bulletin of the Oxford Institute of Statistics .

United Kingdom   1956

Macro-economic level

Purpose

To estimate value of unpaid household services, in relation to national product.

Method
Value of output, at price of market replacement

Cost of keeping adults (30 to 50 inmates) and children (less than 12 inmates) in institutions, for three age groups (less than 5 ; 5 to 14 ; 14 and over), minus expenditures for housing, food and clothing

multiplied by

population in these age groups.

(Evaluation)
(Unpaid household work : ~ 42 per cent of net national product.)

CHAPUT-AUQUIER . 1959

La valeur économique du travail ménager
Cahiers économiques de Bruxelles

Belgium   1956

Macro-economic level

Purpose

"To attempt a gross evaluation of household work, paid and unpaid, in order to relate it to gross national product estimates" (pp. 593 and 595).

Methods
a. Wage, substitute household worker, polyvalent

Time devoted to housework on the basis of limited Belgian information (42 hours per week) and of a French survey (66 hours per week)

multiplied by

houseworker hourly wage.

Comment

"Representative time-use data lacking for Belgium, information was gathered by Dulbea [Brussels' University, Department of Applied Economics] from households presenting average conditions (equipment, three members, etc.) on exclusively that part of housework which can be delegated to unskilled domestic workers: number of hours obtained is therefore an underestimate. French data (Girard, 1958) cover urban families of three members with at least one small child: number of hours thus obtained is overestimated in relation to national average." (pp. 595-6).

(Evaluation) (Housework value: BFR 131,000 to 206,000 million, for a GNP of BFR 513,000 million.)

b. Value of output, at price of market replacement

Cost of keeping children (according to age) and aged people (adults assimilated to the aged) in institutions, minus expenditures for goods and services purchased

multiplied by

population in these categories (cf. 1958, Clark).

(Evaluation) (Housework valued at BFR 147,200 million.)

(Evaluations *a.* and *b.*)

(Housework amounts to approximately 25 to 30 per cent of GNP.)

HIRSCH . 1959

Le "do-it-yourself" dans le cadre de la structure économique
et sociale en Amérique
Le "do-it-yourself" et le commerce

United States   1957

Macro-economic level

Purpose

Assessment of the value of "do-it-yourself" output.

Method

Value of output, based on related consumer expenditures

Assumes "output value must be higher than cost of inputs (raw materials, equipment) as one of the purposes of "do-it-yourself" activity is to save on money expenditures." (p. 40) Analyses consumer expenditures on do-it-yourself inputs.

(Evaluation)

(Do-it-yourself inputs : US $ 7,000 million; output : ~ US $ 10,000 million. Cf GNP : US $ 430,000 million.)

Estimates : 70 to 90 per cent of inside painting, 60 per cent of outside painting, 65 to 80 per cent of wall paper covering, are performed through do-it-yourself.)

GAGE . 1960

The workload and its value for 50 homemakers in Tompkins County, N.Y.

United States   1959

Micro-economic level

Purpose

"To determine the value of the homemaker's contribution and the relation it bears to ... attitudes ... household equipment ... and physical environment" ... (p. 53).

Method

Wage, substitute household worker, specialised (and *Volume of work input, in time* and *Volume of output, by activity*)

Workload expressed in work units (see: 1955, Walker) is determined by survey of 50 households including full-time homemaker with no more than high-school education, husband present, no child under school age; work units are

multiplied by

wage plus fringe benefits of substitute household workers (general housework : US $ 1.22 ; meal preparation : US $ 1.83 ; child care : US $ 0.50).

(Evaluation)

(Household work valued at US $5.93 per day.)

WEISBROD . 1961

Economics of Public Health

United States   ~ 1951

Macro-economic level

Purpose

Measuring the economic loss resulting from mortality by disease.

Method

Wage, substitute household worker, polyvalent (and *Volume of output, by activity*)

"Our approach ... is to determine the present value of the production which the deceased would have contributed (i.e. the income he would have earned) less what he would have consumed, had he not died" (p. 48).

"The value of the average female's household production is determined in relation to the number of other persons (termed "responsibility units", RU) in the family ... by estimating the wages and fringe benefits for a replacing housekeeper when RU = 0 or = 1 or = 3 ; plotted on a chart, these three points are connected by a smooth curve." (pp. 56 and 114).

"The value of household production by age of female is determined on the basis of an estimate of RU at each age".

MACHLUP . 1962

The production and distribution of knowledge in the
United States

United States   1956-1958

Macro-economic level

Purpose

To assess the "private and social cost of women staying at home to take care of a preschool child" (p. 54).

Method
Average wages of females

"Number of women with children of preschool age, not in the labor force, who would potentially be gainfully employed if their labor force participation rate was the same as that of women with children between 6 and 17" (pp. 54-56)

multiplied by

median wage of working women (p. 56).

Comment

"Women who stay at home can do other valuable things in addition to just bringing up their children. Thus the cost of education in the home is really less than the earnings forgone by the mothers ... points to possible overestimation ... but no way of finding out just what corrections should properly be made ..." (note 3, pp. 56-57).

(Evaluation)

(Social cost of women staying at home : $\sim$ US $ 4,400 million in one year.)

MORGAN, DAVID, COHEN and BRAZER . 1962

Income and welfare in the United States

United States   1959

Micro-economic level

Purpose

To determine "the value of the labor put into productive use around the home ... for producing homegrown foods, home additions and repairs ... (housekeeping and child care are not included) ... home production which is a substitute for something which would otherwise have to be purchased ... [Evaluation made] in order to achieve some comparability between spending units in relation to welfare policy" (p. 95).

Method
Value of output, at price of market replacement

Subjective estimate by the producer of the expenses forgone (question asked in the course of social survey "How much did you save by doing these things yourself?").

Comment

"Only crucial home production ... (growing radishes) ... not broad definition of production as a creation of utility ... (growing roses)" (p. 95).

(Evaluation)

(50 per cent of spending units reported some saving of this kind. Average value: US $370 per spending unit, per year.)

FOURASTIE . 1965

Les 40.000 heures

France   1958

Macro-economic level

Purpose

Comparison of time devoted to household unpaid work and to market work.

Method

Volume of work inputs, in time

Evaluation based on time-use study of urban married women (Girard, 1958).

(Evaluation)

(Housework consumed as many hours of work, in 1958, in France as the whole market sector.) (p. 207)

MORGAN, SIRAGELDIN and BAERWALDT . 1966

**Productive Americans : a study of how individuals
contribute to economic progress**

United States   1965

Micro-economic level

Purpose

To evaluate the contribution of "economically productive work done for purposes other than
monetary rewards" (p. 5).

Method
Volume of work inputs, in time

"Measurement of aggregate hours of input devoted to all such activities (p. 102) ... by all
household members (p. 103 ; fig. 8-1) ... [Includes] time devoted to regular housework (meal
preparation, regular cleaning, child care, etc.) (p. 102) and home production (sewing, canning,
gardening, repairing, etc.) (p. 125)" as globally perceived by respondent (interview survey,
representative national sample).

(Evaluation)

(On the average, American families spend four hours per week on home production (p. 125).
The hours devoted to work for money exceed by ~ six per cent the hours devoted to housework.
If home production is added, the hours devoted to unpaid work for self-consumption slightly
exceed (three per cent) the hours devoted to work for money.)

("We estimate that such unpaid work in 1964, if it could be measured, would be found to have
increased the country's estimated Gross National Product by 38 per cent" (p. 5). (Method not
explained in Morgan, 1966 ; but Morgan, in Michel, 1978, p. 213 refers to the use of an average
wage-base of US $ 3/hour).)

HONKANEN . 1967

Kotitaloustyön hinnoitelun perusteista.
Kotitalous
(Quoted in : Kilpiö, 1981a, pp. 29-30)

Finland   1963

Macro-economic level

Purpose

To determine imputed wage for unpaid household work.

Method
Wage, market equivalent function

Time devoted to various household tasks by rural housewives and housewives belonging to the industrial working population ("an extremely limited data sample")

multiplied by

wages of corresponding market jobs (cooks, cleaners, nursemaids, nurses, seamstresses and home economics teachers).

(Evaluation)

(Housework valued at 2.60 FMK/hour in rural families; 3.15 FMK/hour in families of industrial working population. N.B.: no market wage given, in quotation, to permit comparison.)

STUEBLER et al. . 1967

Beiträge zur Arbeitsbewertung in hauswirtschaft-
lichen Tätigkeitsbereichen
Hauswirtschaft und Wissenschaft
(Quoted in : Nederlandse Gezinsraad, 1972)

Federal Republic of Germany   1967

Micro-economic level

Purpose

To acquire insights on the value of housework.

Method
Market equivalent qualifications

Functional analysis technique : analyses skill requirements, responsibility, work hardship and work conditions for 12 household tasks (management, purchasing, feeding, upkeep of premises, etc.); tasks are weighted according to time-costs. Data are combined in job evaluations which vary from one household to another.

MANNING . 1968

Time-use in household tasks by Indiana families

United States   ~ 1961

Micro-economic level

Purpose

... "to obtain quantitative measures of household work and to include quality of performance in the measure ... e.g., in care of master bedroom, 24 per cent of time variability is accounted for by housekeeping standards" (p. 7).

Method

Volume of work inputs, in time and *Volume of output, by activity*

Computes "predictors" of time cost, which like "work units" (see Warren, 1938, Wiegand, 1953 and Walker, 1955) express the average quantity of work accomplished in a certain activity, in a unit of time. Based on a social survey of urban and rural households in which the wives were not employed.

SHAMSEDDINE . 1968

GNP imputations of the value of housewives' services
Economic and Business Bulletin

United States   1950-1964

Macro-economic level

Purpose

"To compare the social accounts of economies at different levels of monetarization methods must be developed to permit comparisons of non-monetized real changes in levels of economic activity" (p. 52) ... attempt to measure magnitude of a very important part of the unpaid economic activities of the American economy" ... (p. 60).

Method
Wage, substitute household worker, specialised

Average time (Walker, 1955 and General Electric, 1952 surveys) devoted by housewives to six categories of homemaking tasks (covering 70 to 75 per cent of total housework in 1955 ; less in 1964) ; average time adjusted for family size, number and age of children, etc., and housewife's employment/non-employment

multiplied by

average wage rates (U.S. Dept. of Labor) for female domestic workers corresponding to three aggregate categories of housework.

Comment

Homemaking tasks covered include meal preparation, dishwashing, regular care of the house, physical care of the children and other family members, washing and ironing. Do not include : chauffeuring, bookkeeping, secretarial service, entertaining, shopping, etc. because satisfactory data are not available. These 25 to 30 per cent left out are mentioned to increase in relative importance with time, but are not evaluated. Because of the magnitude of this unknown element and because of its increasing with time, because also of all the approximations involved in the evaluation, the differences between the 1950 and 1964 evaluations do not appear significant.

(Evaluation)

(The homemaking tasks covered in the study amount to 29,5 per cent of the reported GNP in 1950, and to 24,1 per cent in 1964.)

PYUN . 1969

The monetary value of a housewife : an economic analysis
for use in litigation.
American Journal of Economics and Sociology

United States   1969

Micro-economic level

Purpose

"To develop a workable basis for estimating the monetary value of replacement costs of a
housewife, the purpose of the estimation being to aid judicial decision" (p. 272).

Method

Forgone wage and *Wage, substitute household worker, specialised*

... "estimated prospective earning capacity properly adjusted to the most probable market
value of the replacement costs at going wage rates paid for the usual household occupations ...
[i.e.] adjusted to reconcile a divergence between her earning capacity and her utility creating
capacity for the household" ... (p. 275) ... "adjustment made by the indifference curve
approach" (p. 276).

SIRAGELDIN . 1969

Non-market components of national income

United States   1965

Micro-economic level

Purpose

... "to estimate the value of non-market output (p. 2) ... to discuss the distribution of family incomes and to develop various measures of families' real welfare (p. 4)".

Methods

Time devoted to non-market productive activities at home (Morgan et al., 1966)

multiplied by

a. *Wage, substitute household worker, specialised* and *Wage, market equivalent function*

   average market price of labour performing the same type of activity

b. *Forgone wage*

   reported average hourly earnings, net of taxes and adjusted to account for journey to work (also corrected for "non-equilibrium" conditions: sickness, unemployment, dissatisfaction with the institutional constraints on time allocation).

Comments

"In using market costs [wages], we imply that families occasionally employ servants, domestic help, and other personal services for the home as such" ... (pp. 7-8). In a, the value of an hour spent doing housework is estimated at US $ 1.31; for painting and repairs, US $ 2.44; sewing and mending, US $ 1.79; growing food, canning, freezing, US $ 1.08 In b, "we are assuming that reported average hourly earnings could be used as an approximation for marginal hourly earnings" (p. 22).

(Evaluation)

When using the forgone wage method b, the "average value of unpaid output for the American family is estimated at US $ 3,929 or about 50 per cent of its disposable income" (p. 53). "About 90 per cent of it is in the form of housework and other types of home production" (p. 54). By method a, the value arrived at is 12 per cent lower than with forgone wage on the average, but higher for low income families and vice-versa" (p. 74).

KREPS . 1971

Sex in the market place : American women at work.

United States   1960

Macro-economic level

Purpose

To establish a "rough estimate of the opportunity costs of wives' non-market work" (p. 69) and, as a longer term goal, to "improve the measure of growth in real output and ... change the attitudes of women towards market and non-market work" (p. 68) ... "effect on GNP if ... non-working wives ... came to be employed in market jobs".

Method
Forgone wage

Number of married women, outside the labour force

multiplied by

earnings of employed wives, by age and educational level.

Comment

"Maximum value placed on non-working wife's services can be deducted from the salary that does in fact induce her to take a job" (p. 66).

(Evaluation)

("Forgone earnings of married women outside the labor force and who could theoretically have taken jobs" (pp. 72-73) would have increased the 1960 GNP of over one-sixth.)

LACASSE . 1971

Women at home : the cost to the Canadian economy of
the withdrawal from the labour force of a major proportion
of the female population

Canada   1961

Macro-economic level

Purposes

a. "assessment of the contribution to the Canadian economy, of the non-employed or
part-time employed female population through domestic tasks" (pp. 22-23)

b. estimate of the potential contribution of this population to the production of marketable
goods and services, were these women employed in the same proportion as men.

c. cost to the Canadian economy.

Methods

"arbitrary" (p. 23) estimate of total hours spent on housework

multiplied by

a. Wage, substitute household worker, specialised

average wages of housekeepers, cooks, etc., including and excluding baby-sitters (not
weighted according to use of time for different tasks)

b. Average wages of females

average female wage rates

c. evaluation *b.* minus evaluation *a.*

(Evaluations)

(*a.* Housework is valued 10 to 16 per cent of GNP
b. Potential market contribution : 16 to 22 per cent of GNP
c. Cost to Canadian economy : 6 to 12 per cent.)

CHASE MANHATTAN BANK . 1972

What is a wife worth?

United States   1972

Micro-economic level

Method
Wage, market equivalent function

Number of hours spent at different tasks (99.6 hours/week)

multiplied by

wages paid for the performance of these tasks in the market sector (nursemaid, US $ 2; dietitian, US $ 4.50; food buyer, US $ 3.50; cook, US $ 3.25; dishwasher, US $ 2; housekeeper, US $ 3.25; chauffeur, US $ 3.25; etc.).

Comment

99.6 hours/week because of double-counting of time devoted to overlapping tasks.

(Evaluation)

(Value of a wife : US $ 257.53 per week.)

NEDERLANDSE GEZINSRAAD . 1972

De economische waarde van het voeren van een gezinshuishouding.

Netherlands   1971

Micro-economic level

Purpose

"To arrive at a reasonable and usable assessment of the economic value of homemaking; to find a method taking into account the nature of homemaking functions and the time devoted to them, market wages for similar functions, and money wages forgone in the market by the homemaker."

Method

Market equivalent qualifications and *Wage, substitute household worker* and *Forgone wage*

Wage of "family aid", adjusted for family size (particularly children) and for homemaker educational level.

Comment

Several "reasonable and arbitrary decisions" (p. 12): job analysis weighted by time-use data (Stübler, 1967) of homemaker's tasks points at important share of theoretical knowledge required and of responsibility; wage scale of family aid is therefore used rather than domestic servant's; no job analysis of family aid, however, is available for comparison; selection, within this wage scale, of different values to account for different family sizes; imputation of a higher value for housework performed by a more educated woman, with a weighting factor set at one fourth of what it would be if full differences in opportunity costs were used.

(Evaluation)

(Annual values ranging from HFL 8.000 for family without children, homemaker with primary education only, to HFL 23.000 for family with more than two children, homemaker with higher education. N.B.: ~ HFL 8.000 is reported to be the average wage of 35 year old women, with primary education only, in industry, bank and insurance; HFL 23.000 is the average wage of women with higher education, aged 40.)

NORDHAUS and TOBIN . 1972

Is growth obsolete?

Economic growth

United States   1929-1965

Macro-economic level

Purpose

... "to construct a primitive and experimental 'measure of economic welfare (MEW)' in which we attempt to allow for the more obvious discrepancies between GNP and economic welfare" ... (p. 4) ... "adjustments to GNP ... for the product of household work ..." (p. 5).

Method
Average wages of females

Time devoted to housework according to a 1954 survey of "doubtful reliability" (p. 43)

multiplied by

average hourly wages adjusted for sex, employment status, etc., and deflated by the average wage rates (alternative one) or by the consumer price index (alternative two, preferred by the authors).

Comments

"The basic issue is whether the consumption prices of non-market uses of time have (a) risen with wage rates or (b) risen with the prices of market consumption goods ... (p. 39) ... ; three possible deflators for housework : wage index, or total consumption deflator, or its service component ... (p. 42) ... The wage index rose twice as fast as the two others between 1929 and 1965 ... The essential question is whether non-market activities have shared in the technical progress that has raised real wages." (p. 40).

Reliability of the estimates : "... the official estimates of the unreliability of GNP ... in the United Kingdom, is that three percentage points either way include a 90 per cent confidence interval (Maurice, 1969, pp. 42 and 52) ... estimate the error on non-market activity in MEW to be about ten times the percentage error of GNP." (p. 59).

(Evaluation)

(Using the consumer price index as deflator, non-market household activity is evaluated for 1929 at US $ 85,700 million i.e. 42 per cent of GNP ; for 1965 at US $ 295,400 million i.e. 48 per cent of GNP.)

SCOTT . 1972

The value of housework ; for love or for money?
Ms Magazine

(Quotations are found in the literature to an evaluation by A.C. Scott. In fact this is not an original evaluation; Scott (1972, p. 56) is referring to the 1972 Chase Manhattan Bank evaluation.)

*

*　　*

GALBRAITH . 1973

Economics and the public purpose

(Quotations are found in the literature to an evaluation by J.K. Galbraith. In fact this is not an original evaluation; Galbraith (1973, p. 33) is quoting A.C. Scott, 1972.)

GRONAU . 1973a

The intrafamily allocation of time:
the value of the housewives' time

American Economic Review

United States   1960

Micro-economic level

Purpose

To "attempt a general formulation of the intrafamily allocation of time ... according to comparative advantage in production of market and home goods" (p. 634).

Method

Forgone wage

From labour market behaviour i.e. participation or not in labour force (p. 645) as given from 1960 Census, and accounting for race, family income, children less than three years old, etc., derives value placed by the family on the wife's time:

a.   if in the labour force, wife's time is valued at her own wage rate;

b.   if leaves the labour market, her price is determined by family income. Two interpretations: "Wives who work are those who: 1) are the least productive in the home sector ... hence mean price of time of housework exceeds the average wage rate of working women; 2) have received the highest wage offers and hence the mean price of time falls short of the average wage rate" (p. 635);

c.   if husband enters home production process, her price is determined by his wage rate (p. 635).

Comments

"Work, whether in the market or in the non-market sector, is assumed explicitly as carrying no utility (or disutility)" (p. 635).

"Common practice to equate value of time of housewives with that of working wives ... may involve an error of close to 20 per cent in the case of white housewives ... and up to 50 per cent in the case of non-white women" (p. 650).

GRONAU . 1973b

The measurement of output of the non-market sector :
the evaluation of housewives' time

The measurement of economic and social performance

Israel   1969

Micro-economic level

Purpose

To establish an ... "estimation of the price of time of the non-employed ... housewives" (p. 166).

Methods

Average wages of females and *Forgone wage*

From "rate of labor force participation and average wage rate derives an interval estimate of the mean price of time", accounting for age, education, husband's income, presence of small children. (p. 183) Based on a model in which "for those units of time which are freely substitutable for work in the market, the value of time depends on the net marginal wage rate" (p. 170).

Comment

Two interpretations : see Gronau, 1973a, method *b*.

(Evaluation)

("Interpretation 1) : value of housewives' time exceeds the average wage rate of working women by no more than 5 per cent. Interpretation 2) : value of housewives' time is $\sim$ 80 per cent of women's average wage rate ... (p. 168) ... The housewife's price of time increases with husband's income ... elasticity 0.30 to 0.50 ... No evidence of effect of young children ..." (p. 168).)

JAPAN, ECONOMIC COUNCIL . 1973

Measuring net national welfare in Japan
(Quoted in : Saunders, 1976)

Japan   1955-1970

Macro-economic level

Purpose

"... experimental effort to construct ... an alternative set of accounts leading up to an aggregated measure of 'welfare' expressed in monetary terms ... (p. 6) ... to supplement GNP's function in the welfare aspect" (p. 4).

Method
Average wages of females

Number of full-time housewives (Labour Force Survey)

multiplied by

average number of hours spent on housework (Survey of People's Living Hours 1960 ; 48.7 hours per week in 1960 ; 45.6 hours in 1970)

multiplied by

average hourly wage earnings of females.

Comment

For comparison of results with United States between 1919 and 1965 (Nordhaus and Tobin, 1972), see Saunders (1976, p. 19).

(Evaluation)

(Housework evaluated at 11.2 per cent of GNP, in 1955 ; 8.7 per cent in 1970.)

LINDGREN . 1974

Kotitaloustyön arvo ; työaikatutkimukseen perustuva arviointiyritys
(Quoted in : Kilpiö, 1981a)

Finland   1973

Macro-economic level

Purpose

To estimate the total value of housework in relation to GNP.

Method
Wage, substitute household worker, polyvalent

Estimate of time devoted to children of different ages, in families of different sizes multiplied by
 number of families of each type

multiplied by

average hourly wages of municipal housekeepers

minus

estimate of child care provided outside the home

plus

estimate of time devoted to other housework.

Comment

Subjective estimates constitute the basis of the evaluation.

(Evaluation)

(Housework is evaluated at FMK 10,600 million i.e. ~ 16 per cent of GNP.)

ROSEN . 1974

The monetary value of a housewife :
a replacement cost approach

American Journal of Economics and Sociology

United States   1974

Micro-economic level

Purpose

"... to aid economists in the courtroom ..." (p. 71).

Method

Wage, substitute household worker, polyvalent

Value of a housewife : when she achieves "equilibrium", her time is distributed between market work (which yields her monetary value), homework (non-monetary value, valued at replacement cost by a professional homemaker) and leisure ; her value is obtained after deduction of her personal consumption.

Comment

Choice in time-allocation is made on the basis of utility maximisation, but housework is valued at substitute household worker's wage.

WEINROBE . 1974

Household production and national production :
an improvement of the record

Review of Income and Wealth

United States   1960-1970

Macro-economic level

Purpose
Average wages of females

To "present estimates of the value of homebased non-market production by housewives ... estimates then used to supplement various national product aggregates in order to calculate more accurate growth rates for the U.S. economy ..." (p. 89).

Method
Time devoted to household production by full-time and part-time homemakers, and by gainfully employed wives (Walker, 1970)

multiplied by

median female earnings.

Comment
Time data are the same for the whole period. Year to year variations of the estimated values do not reflect variations in the volume of household product, but variations in "the relative rate at which median wages were rising relative to the national product" (p. 99).

(Evaluation)
(Value of homebased non-market production by housewives is $\sim$ 30 per cent of the GNP and $\sim$ 40 per cent of the national income.)

ARVEY and BEGALLA . 1975

Analyzing the homemaker job using the position analysis questionnaire (PAQ)

Journal of Applied Psychology

United States   1968-9 and 1974

Micro-economic level

Purpose

"To determine if the [homemaker] job is amenable to analysis, to associate a wage with the job, to identify closely related jobs, to examine correlates (such as age, ...); to serve as a starting point for further research and investigation." (p. 517).

Method
Wage, market equivalent qualifications

"Position analysis questionnaire, submitted to 50 homemakers to measure behaviours and psychological processes involved in the job. Then homemaker job profile is compared with a sample of 531 market jobs, to estimate income value." (p. 514)

Comment

"This wage rate seems to be overinflated compared to our general notions of the job compared to other jobs ... due to tendencies on the part of the subjects to depict aspects of their jobs as being perhaps more important than they might in fact be ... (p. 516) ... [due also to the interviewing of] higher income-bracket individuals (p. 517). The authors do not wish this wage rate to be quoted out of context without careful attention to possible biases and artifacts involved in this research."

(Evaluation)

(Monthly wage value of homemaker job: 1968-9, US $ 740; 1974: US $ 991. Patrolman: greatest profile similarity. Lower socio-economic level subjects, the older and the less educated described their job as less important or less complex.)

BRODY . 1975

Economic value of a housewife

Research and Statistics Note

United States   1972

Micro-economic level

Purpose

"... in order to determine the total economic cost of disease, the economic value of the various members of society must be measured in terms of their productivity ..." (p. 1).

Methods

a. Wage, market equivalent functions

"The average value of a woman of a given age, with a given number of children and given age of youngest child (Walker and Gauger, 1973) was weighted by the percent of women" (p. 4) in the total United States population, not employed and sharing these characteristics.

b. Average wages of females

Number of full-time homemakers, multiplied by average earnings of women employed full-time

Wage, substitute household worker, polyvalent

Number of full-time homemakers, multiplied by wages of full-time domestic workers.

(Evaluation)

(Average annual economic value of a housewife : between US $ 3,935 and US$ 4,705.)

HEGELAND . 1975

Barn, kvinnor, hemarbete
(Quoted in : Kilpiö, 1981a)

Sweden   1973

Macro-economic level

Purpose

To estimate time devoted to children at home.

Method

Volume of work inputs, in time

Estimate of time devoted to children of different ages, in families of different sizes. (A child 0-3 years old is estimated to require 52 hours per week for physical and material care, active togetherness and child supervision. Time required is assumed to decrease with age; 10-18 years old: 12 hours per week. Time is assumed not to increase proportionately with the number of children; it is assumed to increase by 50 per cent for each subsequent child)

multiplied by

number of families of each type.

Comment

Evaluation based on subjective estimates of time inputs.

JAPAN, SUPREME COURT . 1975

Decision, Hanrei Jiho

Judicial Decisions Review

Japan   1975

Micro-economic level

Purpose

Ruling on wife's household work ; evaluation of wife's contribution to household income, for use by courts in case of wrongful death, divorce, etc.

Method
Average wages of females

"A wife engaged exclusively in household work yields an economic gain equivalent to the average wage of women workers, until she reaches the age of incapacity for work".

KREDIETBANK . 1975

La femme dans l'économie

Bulletin hebdomadaire

Belgium   1972

Macro-economic level

Purpose

Evaluation of women's contribution to national income.

Method
Average wages of females

Number of full-time housewives, multiplied by 46 hours of housework per week (based on time-use surveys ; no reference given)

plus

number of gainfully employed wives with family responsibilities, multiplied by 30 hours of housework per week

total, multiplied by

average hourly wage of gainfully employed women.

(Evaluation)

(Net national income :   ∼ BFR 1,262,000 million
Housework :   ∼ BFR   508,000 million, i.e. 40 per cent of net national income.
Total :   ∼ BFR 1,780,000 million, of which

housework	29 per cent
gainfully employed contribution,	
women	14 per cent
men	46 per cent
capital returns	11 per cent.)

RUGGLES and RUGGLES . 1975

The measurement of economic and social performance

Paper, 14th Conference, International Association for Research in Income and Wealth
(Quoted in : Saunders, 1976)

United States   1948-1969

Macro-economic level

Purpose

... "estimation of a number of welfare-oriented variables ... not aiming at an aggregate described as a measure of welfare ... permit the measurement of a concept of 'extended gross national product' ... " (p. 8).

Method

Wage, substitute household workers, specialised or *Wage, market equivalent functions?*

Time devoted to housework (based on a collection of time budgets, adjusted for urban/rural households differences, with and without children, stratified by age of youngest child)

multiplied by

market wages of specialised workers (household workers or workers in business enterprises, not clear from quotation).

(Evaluation)

(Unpaid household work is evaluated, for 1948, at 34.3 per cent of GNP (current prices) and for 1969, at 29.5 per cent.)

SCHULZ-BORCK . 1975

Was ist eine Hausfrau wert?

Verbraucher Dienst

Federal Republic of Germany   1973

Micro-economic and macro-economic levels

Purpose

To define ground of housekeepers' remuneration in institutions; to advise courts on value of housewife's services lost in cases of wrongful death; to determine value of housework for scientific purposes.

Methods

a.   Micro-Economic Level   *Market equivalent qualifications*

a.1 Job evaluation techniques used analytically in order to determine responsibilities, qualifications, working conditions, etc.

Comment

"... homemaking is primarily a managerial function; the homemaker continues to be a manager when doing a simple routine task ... all household work should be priced at the level of a manager ..." "In spite of intensive research ... not possible yet to rely on analytical job evaluation techniques for establishing value of homemaker job ..." (p. 84).

a.2 Job evaluation techniques used globally in order to establish equivalence with civil service salary scales.

(Evaluation)

(Housework valued DM 1,500 to 2,300 per month.)

b.   Macro-Economic Level   *Volume of work inputs, in time*

Number of households (23 million) multiplied by average number of hours housewives devote to housework, as given by time-use surveys (45 hours per week)

compared to

number of hours worked by all workers in market sector.

(Evaluation)

(Housewives devoted 53,000 million hours to housework in 1973; work hours in market sector: 55,000 million.)

GRONAU . 1976

Who is the family's main breadwinner?
The wife's contribution to full income

National Bureau Economic Research, Research Paper

United States   1973

Micro-economic level

Purpose

"To assess the contribution of United States white married women to full income, in relation to age, education, number of children in household, employment status".

Method
Forgone wage

"Time devoted to housework ("very loose concept") as given by Michigan Income Dynamics Survey, 1974" (p. 1)

multiplied by

market wage "imputed" (p. 10) from housewife's education, labour force experience and husband's education.

(Evaluation)

("Average value of home production of American wife equals approximately four times her earnings ... wife's household product plus her earnings equal approximately 45 to 50 per cent of the family's gross full income" (p. 3).)

WALKER and WOODS . 1976

Time use : a measure of household production of family goods and services

---

United States   1967-1968

Micro-economic level, for extension to macro-economic

Purpose

... "to find a means of measuring the workload in household production that could be relatively simple to use and for which data could be easily collected ... (p. 246) ... to identify significant variables (p. 248) ... and to express a measure of household work in terms of average time for various types of families" ... (p. 8).

Method

Volume of work inputs, in time and *Volume of output, by activity*

Social survey of 1300 husband and wife households, with and without children in different numbers and ages, in urban-suburban population of Syracuse, New York; measure all household members' household production by the amount of time, primary and secondary, devoted to household work (total and by activity); determine average time for an average worker under average household conditions.

Comment

"Same relationship between time spent and work accomplished as in the case of work units" (p. 9), but "in relation to family composition variables instead of task specific variables" (p. 7) (Cf Walker, 1955 and 1958).

Significant variables are found to be number of children, age of youngest child, wife's employment, etc.

ADRET . 1977

Travailler deux heures par jour

France   1975

Macro-economic level

Purpose

To evaluate the respective quantitative shares of gainful work and of unpaid work in France (p. 116).

Method

Volume of work inputs, in time

Time devoted to unpaid household work (cooking, housecleaning, gardening, child care, shopping, etc.) taken from Lemel, 1974

compared to

hours in gainful employment, taking unemployment into account.

(Evaluation)

(Unpaid household work : 49,000 million hours, of which
                          9,000 million by men
                          40,000 by women
Gainful work :   37,200 million hours, of which
                          24,500 million by men
                          12,700 million by women
Unpaid household work :   ~ 30 per cent more than gainful work.)

DEIST-BOHNER . 1977

Arbeitsbewertung in der Hauswirtschaft
(Quoted in Walker, 1980, pp. 129-130)

Federal Republic of Germany   1977

Micro-economic level

Purpose

"To determine the kinds of industrial jobs that make demands on the worker similar to those on the homemaker".

Method
Market equivalent qualifications

Functional analysis technique: analyse requirements for many household activities in seven households (knowledge, skill, level of responsibility, physical and mental costs, working conditions); then combine into a total job description for comparison with industrial jobs.

Comment

"If used for pricing household work, the wage level for jobs with similar requirements then could be used to estimate the value of time used for household work" (p. 130).

KENDRICK . 1977

**Expanding imputed values in the national income
and product accounts**

Paper, 15th Conference, International Association for Research Income and Wealth
(Quoted in : Murphy, 1979)

United States   1929-1973

Macro-economic level

Purpose

Evaluation of home services in relation to national accounting.

Method

Wage, substitute household workers, specialised or *Wage, market equivalent functions*

Number of hours devoted to various household services (food preparation, service and clean up ; construction and repair ; making of, and caring for, clothing and home furnishings ; care of family including transportation ; household management, record keeping, shopping, etc.)

multiplied by

wages of substitute household workers (or of business enterprise workers? ; not clear from quotation).

ADLER and HAWRYLYSHYN . 1978

Estimates of the value of household work, Canada, 1961-1971

Review of Income and Wealth

Canada   1961-1971

Macro-economic level

Purpose

To estimate imputed dollar value of household work, in relation to GNP.

Methods

a. Wage, market equivalent functions

Average wages for at least two or three occupations equivalent to household functions (no indication of how equivalence is established, but two examples are given "for clothing care, we included ... personal service, janitors, charworkers and cleaners, sewing machine operators, and tailors and dressmakers" (p. 341); "for food preparation, wages of dietitians would yield a 20 per cent higher value, of waitresses and hostesses a 5 per cent lower value than the wage combination used" (p. 342)), adjusted for male/female wage differentials

multiplied by

time devoted to housework disaggregated by sex, type of household, age of children and wife's market status (pp. 336 and 341); time-use data given by surveys in Halifax and Toronto.

b. Wage, substitute household worker, polyvalent

Number of families (?)

multiplied by

housekeeper wages (p. 340).

c. Average wages

Number of families (?)

multiplied by

average wage for males or females, net of taxes (p. 335).

(continued overleaf)

Comment

"Wages are the one variable that has a significant impact on these estimates, and it is therefore imperative that these values be chosen with circumspection" (p. 348).

"The cost-by-function method |"wage, market equivalent functions" in our typology| is preferred because found superior in theoretical support ... but opportunity cost |"wage, substitute household worker, polyvalent" in our typology| gives a good approximation in the aggregate and is simpler" (pp. 333, 340, 348). "Data on housekeeper wages are questionable ... and give an estimate ... significantly lower ..." (p. 340).

(Evaluation)

(Value of housework in 1971 :

a. : 41 per cent of GNP if based on female wages ; 53 per cent of GNP if based on men's wages

b. : 34 per cent of GNP

c. : 40 per cent of GNP.)

CLARKE and OGUS . 1979

What is a wife worth?

British Journal of Law and Society

United Kingdom, mostly, but also Australia, France, Federal Republic of Germany , New Zealand and United States.

Micro-economic level

Purpose

To assess the value of services lost when housewife is injured or killed, and of services gained when she nurses a handicaped member of the family.

Methods

Discusses methods used by courts :

a. Wage, substitute household workers, specialised

b. Forgone wage

c. Value of output, at price of market replacement

cost of care in institutions.

Comments

Points at inconsistencies in method selection, for application to similar cases within the same legal system or in legal and social security systems of the same country, and points at lingering impact of social values about women's roles and the family.

HAUSERMAN and FETHKE . 1978

Valuation of a homemaker's services

Trial Lawyer's Guide

United States   1978

Micro-economic level

Purpose

"To provide a methodological guide for lawyers, for the economic valuation of non-market services of the homemaker ... monetary value of this contribution" (pp. 249-250) in law suits relating to marriage dissolution, wrongful death and personal injury.

Methods

Wage, substitute household workers, specialised and *Wage, market equivalent functions* and *Forgone wage*

Replacement cost by household worker (domestic cook, day worker for house care), market equivalent function (personal service laundry, nurses aid or orderly, bookkeeper) and wage forgone, all adjusted to particular case at hand (size of household, number and age of children, educational level, previous employment, incidence on career development of non-employment because of homemaking, etc.).

Comments

Interesting detailed analysis of some aspects of the interface, at the micro-economic level, between the market and non-market sectors. From the law practice point of view, overlooks social constraints pushing women in low-pay jobs and in housekeeping tasks.

KENDE . 1978

Les biens et les services autoproduits dans la consommation
des ménages français.

Les femmes dans la société marchande

France   1974-1975

Micro-economic level

Purpose

"To determine, from the value added point of view, the 'quasi-monetary value' of household
productive activities" (p. 238). "To assess its importance in relation to available monetary
income and to 'real consumption' ('overall socially valued resources available to a
consumption unit during a defined period of time')" (p. 225).

Method

Wage, substitute household worker, specialised and *Wage, market equivalent function*

Number of hours devoted to housework tasks by all family members in 60 families in the Paris
area (1974-1975 survey), with two to four children, some wives gainfully employed and others
not,

multiplied by

hourly wages in the area for household workers (FF. 10 for houseworker) or market workers
(child care in own home, FF. 3 ; painter : FF. 45, etc.).

Comment

According to goal pursued, "if interested only in the amount of income in kind generated ... a
good evaluation of added value in household production is sufficient ; if interest extends to
human costs or to social organisation externalities, it is appropriate to take into account hours
of work ... time lost ... which reduce the free time at the individual's disposal ..." (p. 237).

MURPHY . 1978

The value of non-market household production :
opportunity cost vs market cost estimates.

Review of Income and Wealth

United States   1960-1970

Macro-economic level

Purpose

Evaluation of non-market household production for comparison with GNP and for welfare assessment.

Methods

Number of hours spent by adults (male and female) on housecleaning, cooking, etc. according to time-use studies (broken down according to employment status of females, marital status, number and age of children)

multiplied by

a. Wage, market equivalent functions

average hourly wage, by sex, of persons performing the market counterpart of the non-market task (food preparation: cooks, not in private households; house upkeep: cleaning service workers; clothing maintenance: laundry and dry-cleaning operatives; family care: private household workers living in; marketing, bookkeeping, household management: housekeepers, not in private households, and accounting clerks class B).

b. Average wages

average hourly wage, by sex, of full-time civilian workers, less income tax.

Comments

Author prefers first method for comparisons with GNP, because output only is counted, not utility, and second method for welfare assessment (pp. 245 and 251).

Larger decline between 1960 and 1970 with first method reflects relatively larger increase of average wages than of wages of occupations selected as equivalent functions.

(Evaluation)

(Non-market household production evaluated with method *a.*: 1960, 36.8 per cent; 1970, 34.3 per cent of GNP. Evaluated with method *b.*: 1960, 37.6 per cent; 1970, 37.1 per cent of GNP.)

116

PROULX . 1978

Cinq millions de femmes ; une étude de la femme canadienne au foyer

---

Canada   1977

Micro-economic level

Purpose

"To illustrate the possibility for every woman to approximately calculate the value of her housework" (p. 50).

Method

Wage, market equivalent function

Application, to one hypothetical example, of the method used by Adler and Hawrylyshyn (1978) at the macro-economic level.

Female wages, averaged for skill levels, as estimated by Adler and Hawrylyshyn for 1971, indexed on cost of living for 1977

multiplied by

time devoted to housework.

Comment

Value obtained is strongly affected by value imputed on tasks absorbing the largest share of household work.

(Evaluation)

(Average value of time for hypothetical example taken : Can. $ 3.82 per hour. No market wage values given which would permit comparisons.)

SCHACHT . 1979

Bemessung und Bewertung des Naturalunterhaltes in der Doppelverdienerehe

---

Federal Republic of Germany   1979

Micro-economic level

Purpose

To provide a guide for the evaluation of housewife's lost services in court cases relating to wrongful death.

Method
Wage, market equivalent function

Average time devoted by housewives to 12 categories of homemaking tasks, adjusted for family size, number and age of children

multiplied by

wages of workers performing similar functions in the market (cook, cook aid, teacher, nursery school teacher, nurse, etc.).

FERBER and BIRNBAUM . 1980

Housework : priceless or valueless?

Review of Income and Wealth

United States   1977

Micro-economic level

Purpose

... "to illustrate ... through selected representative profiles, the impact of changes of several variables on estimates of the value of women's housework." (p. 391) and particularly the impact of labour force participation patterns. The emphasis is thus on methodological considerations.

Methods

The lifetime value of a woman's housework is calculated on the basis of time-use data (Robinson, 1977), taking into account age, education, number of children and pattern of labour force participation.

a. Forgone wage

Estimate is based on actual wages of women with same characteristics (age, etc.) in clerical work at University of Illinois (adjusted for taxes and commuting time).

b. Wage, substitute household worker, polyvalent

Estimate is based on wages of full-time private household workers, adjusted for level of education (1970, Census).

Comments

"Thus we conclude that while potential market earnings ["forgone wage" in our typology] may well be important, or even crucial, in determining how much time a person will devote to market and housework, and while it is true that, in a sense, the cost of housework is market earnings forgone, they do not provide an acceptable estimate of the value of work done in the home ... The market cost approach ["wage, substitute household worker, polyvalent" in our typology] ... does present difficulties of its own ... (p. 395) ... [but] it is preferable to the opportunity cost approach, and using the wages of general household workers is clearly preferable than using those of specialists" (p. 399).

(Evaluation)

("... Using opportunity cost [*a.*], we find the life-time value of housework of the high school graduate who spends ten years as a full-time homemaker, is little higher than that of the woman who works full-time in the labor-market throughout and spends considerably less time on housework than the former ..." (p. 394).)

GAUGER and WALKER . 1980

The dollar value of household work
(Revised version of Walker and Gauger, 1973a)

United States   1979

Micro-economic and macro-economic levels

Purpose

To assist families in the assessment of the dollar value of household work they perform, e.g. for time allocation decisions (pp. 2 and 10); to assist experts in the assessment of family losses in accidents, injuries and divorce proceedings (p. 2); to evaluate household work in relation to GNP.

Method
Wage, market equivalent function and *Minimum legal wage*

Time devoted to housework (sample surveys in Syracuse, New York 1967-68 and 1977) by wives, husbands and teen agers, by category of tasks (marketing, management and record keeping, food preparation and aftermeal cleanup, housecare and maintenance, yard and car care, etc.), taking into account number of children, age of youngest child, employment status of wife

multiplied by

wage rates (1979) of "workers in the market place who perform services similar to household tasks" (p. 7) (kitchen helper, $ 3.02; housekeeper, $ 3.18; laundry worker, $ 3.20; yard worker, $ 3.21, child care worker (not specialised in child development), $ 3.50; homemaker aide, $ 3.50; cook, $ 3.58; dressmaker, $ 4.48; cleaning person, $ 4.75) and legal minimum wages for teenagers; fringe benefits not included; income taxes not accounted for.

Comment

"Conservative estimate: ... what it would cost to hire someone to do the task, not ... to replace the family member ... difficult for the relatively small amounts of time" (pp. 7-8).

(Evaluation)

(Average annual value of housework in a family with two teenage children; if the wife is non-employed: US $ 14,500; if the wife is employed: US $ 10,500 per year.)

120

GRONAU . 1980

Home production ; a forgotten industry

Review of Economics and Statistics

United States   1973

Micro-economic level

Purpose

Measurement of total home output (not of value added).

Method

Forgone wage

A production function equation is derived from a utility maximising model, and applied to data from the Michigan Study of Income Dynamics (1974), which includes data on income, education, family composition, etc. as well as time devoted to loosely defined housework.

(Evaluation)

(Average annual value of housework for white married women sample : US $ 7,587, i.e. 70 per cent of the family's money income after taxes or 60 per cent before taxes.)

SUVIRANTA and HEINONEN . 1980

The value of unsalaried home care of children
under the age of seven in 1979

Housework Study

Finland   1979

Macro-economic level

Purpose

Evaluation of unsalaried home care of children under the age of seven.

Method

Volume of output, by activity and *Volume of work inputs, in time*
and *Wage, market equivalent function*

Volume of home care of children, expressed in time ("time when children are at home at the same time with and under the control of some older member of the household ... active and passive child care ... up to 24 hours a day ..." (pp. 47-49), adjusted for age of children and family size (cf Hegeland, 1975)) as given by sample survey (Part II of same study)

multiplied by

wage of a "municipal child minder" at day rates (active child care) and night rates (passive child care), plus fringe benefits

total, minus

paid day care.

(Evaluation)

(Unsalaried home care of children under seven evaluated at 5.7 per cent of GNP.)

BERGMANN . 1981

The economic risks of being a housewife

American Economic Review

United States   1973

Micro-economic level

Purpose

... "to estimate what the housewife receives as return for her work ... almost all the pay takes the form of non-cash benefits ... room, board, clothing allowance, medical care, all-expenses paid vacations, [etc.]" (p. 83).

Method

Wage in kind and *Value of output, based on related consumer expenditures*

... "using a scheme in which a man's expenditure for his own clothing is taken to be an index of his standard of living ..." (p. 83).

Comments

See 4.2.2 and 5.2 in Chapters 4 and 5 above.

(Evaluation)

("Cost of a housewife to a child-free married man : about half of his pay ..." A child-free married man "needs twice the income of a single man in order to afford the same clothing expenditures" (p. 83).

BUND SCHWEIZERISCHER FRAUENORGANISATIONEN und
BETRIEBSWISSENSCHAFTLICHES INSTITUT DER
EIDGENÖSSISCHEN TECHNISCHEN HOCHSCHULE ZÜRICH . 1981

Wertschätzung der Haushaltarbeit

Switzerland   1980

Micro-economic level

Purpose

Job evaluation.

Method
Market equivalent qualifications

Analysis of 65 different types of households, representative of the majority of Swiss households (according to number of household members, housing, income level, etc.). Activities covered include gardening, animal care, hospitality for a meal or overnight, etc., in addition to regular housework. Responsibility, commitment, mental or physical effort, etc. are rated on a 1.000 point scale ; rating criteria defined and weighted by an ad-hoc committee.

Comment

No comparison with market sector jobs.

SUVIRANTA and MYNTTINEN . 1981

The value of unpaid housecleaning in 1980

Housework study

Finland 1980

Macro-economic level

Purpose

... "To calculate the value of unpaid housecleaning ... regular and special ... done by household members in their own homes ..." (p. 35).

Method

Volume of output, by activity and *Value of output, at price of market replacement*

Volume of housecleaning, expressed in square meters of dwelling area, as given by sample survey (Part II of same study)

multiplied by

cost per square meter for cleaning day-care centers (direct and indirect labour costs and management costs only, i.e. 86 per cent of total cleaning costs; derived from "... a very thorough computation ... carried out by the bureau in charge of planning cleaning work for the City of Helsinki ... of costs of cleaning in institutions ...; children day care centers ... considered to correspond in large measure to home conditions — especially homes with children — with regard to the type of rooms, the amount of time spent in them and other characteristics ..." (p. 35)

total, minus

paid cleaning help, as given by sample survey; time valued at "average labour costs for cleaners employed by the City of Helsinki" (p. 36).

Value thus obtained, divided by average time spent in cleaning (survey) gives imputed average wage for housecleaning.

(continued overleaf)

Comment

Direct and indirect labour costs constituting the largest portion of costs (86 per cent; p. 35), the imputed household wage comes close to the wage of a cleaner employed by the city. The difference may be attributable to a certain lack of correspondence between cleaning day-care centers and households, perhaps to differences in cleaning standards and in equipment, and to approximations in reporting time devoted to household cleaning. This equivalence holds because cleaning is a labour intensive activity. This study indicates that, for this particular labour-intensive task, city wages could have been used as the basis of the evaluation (Wage, market equivalent function).

Scale economies which may occur, in the remaining 14 per cent of city costs, through wholesale purchasing of equipment and materials, intensive amortisation of equipment, access to repair workshops, etc., are not highlighted, as they are left out of the calculation.

(Evaluation)

(Imputed housecleaning wage: FMK 11.76; city cleaner wage, before tax: FMK 14.71. Housecleaning aggregate value: 3.9 per cent of GNP.)

BIBLIOGRAPHY

The publications listed below are relevant to the subject of this study and were consulted in the course of its preparation. No attempt was made at documenting every statement in the study. Quotations and references are therefore kept to a minimum in the main body of the study while they are used extensively in the appendix summaries.

Adler, H.J.; Hawrylyshyn, O. 1978. "Estimates of the value of household work, Canada 1961 and 1971", in *Review of Income and Wealth* (New Haven, Conn.), Dec. 1978, pp. 333-355.

Andrews, B.J. 1935. *Economics of the household: Its administration and finance.* New York, Macmillan.

Adret. 1977. *Travailler deux heures par jour.* Collection Points, Série Actuels. Paris, Seuil.

Arvey, R.O.; Begalla, M.E. 1975. "Analyzing the homemaker job, using the position analysis questionnaire (PAQ)", in *Journal of Applied Psychology* (Washington, DC), Vol. 60, No. 4, pp. 513-517.

Ashenfelter, O.; Heckman, J. 1974. "The estimation of income and substitution effects in a model of family labor supply", in *Econometrica* (Evanston, Ill.), Jan. 1974, pp. 73-85.

Becker, G.S. 1965. "A theory of the allocation of time", in *Economic Journal* (Cambridge), Sep. 1965, pp. 493-517.

———. 1976. *The economic approach to human behavior.* Chicago, University of Chicago Press.

Bergmann, B.R. 1981. "The economic risks of being a housewife", in *American Economic Review* (Nashville, Tenn.), May 1981, pp. 81-86.

Berk, R.A. 1980. "The new home economics: An agenda for sociological research", in S.F. Berk (ed.): *Women and household labor,* op. cit., pp. 113-148.

———; Berk, S.F. 1978. "A simultaneous equation model for the division of household labor", in *Sociological Methods and Research* (Beverly Hills, Calif.), Vol. 6, No. 4, pp. 431-468.

Berk, S.F. (ed.). 1980. *Women and household labor.* Sage yearbooks in women's policy studies; Vol. 5. Beverly Hills, Calif. and London, Sage.

Beutler, I.F.; Owen, A.J.. 1980. "New perspectives on home production: A conceptual view", in C. Hefferan (ed.): *The household as producer: A look beyond the market,* op. cit., pp. 15-30.

Brody, W.H. 1975. *Economic value of a housewife*. Research and statistics note No. 9; DHEW Pub. No. SSA 75-11701. Washington, DC, United States Department of Health, Education and Welfare.

Brown (Vickery), C. 1981. "Home production for use in a market economy", in B. Thorne (ed.) : *Rethinking the family : Some feminist questions*, op. cit.

Bund Schweizerischer Frauenorganisationen und Betriebswissenschaftliches Institut Der Eidgenössischen Technischen Hochschule Zürich. 1981. *Wertschätzung der Haushaltarbeit*. Zürich. Mimeographed.

Burns, S. 1977. *The household economy*. Boston, The Beacon Press.

Cannon. 1928. *The family finances of 195 farm families in Tompkins County, New York, 1927-8*. Agricultural Experiment Station bulletin, 522. Ithaca, N.Y.

Chapman, J.R. (ed.). 1976. *Economics independence for women : The foundation for equal rights*. Sage yearbooks in women's policy studies, Vol. 1. London, Sage.

Chaput-Auquier, G. 1959. "La valeur économique du travail ménager", in *Cahiers économiques de Bruxelles* (Brussels), July 1959, pp. 593-600.

Chase Manhattan Bank. 1972. *What is a wife worth?* New York. Mimeographed.

Christelijke Sociale Vrouwenwerkers; Christelijke Arbeiders Vrouwengilden. [1951?]. *Economische waarde van de huishoudelijke taak der vrouw*. Brussels. Mimeographed.

Clark, C. 1958. "The economics of housework", in *Bulletin of the Oxford Institute of Statistics* (Oxford), May 1958, pp. 205-211.

———. 1971. "Le travail ménager et le produit national", in *Analyse et Prévision*, June 1971, pp. 759-771. (Translation of Clark, 1958.)

Clarke, K.A. ; Ogus, A.I. 1978. "What is a wife worth?", in *British Journal of Law and Society* (Cardiff, UK), Summer 1978, pp. 1-25.

Cogan, J.F. 1975. "Married women's labor supply: A comparison of alternative estimation procedures", in J. Smith (ed.): *Female labor supply: theory and estimation*, op. cit.

Danmark, Statistiske Department. 1948. "Nationalproduktet og nationalindkomsten 1930-1946", in *Statistiske Meddelelser* (Copenhagen), Series 4, Vol. 129, Fasc. 5.

———. 1951. "Nationalproduktet og nationalindkomsten 1946-1949", in *Statistiske Meddelelser* (Copenhagen), Series 4, Vol. 140, Fasc. 2.

Dayre, J. 1955. "Habitat, services résidentiels et niveau de vie", in *Etudes et Documents du Centre de Recherches économiques et sociales* (Paris), May 1955, pp. 1-64.

De Groote, J. 1974. "Le travail ménager et le revenu national", in *Cahiers du GRIF* (Brussels), Feb. 1974, pp. 21-24.

Deist-Bohner, H. 1977. *Arbeitsbewertung in der Hauswirtschaft*. München, Verlag Lipp.

Le *"do-it-yourself"* et le commerce. 1959. Proceedings of the Seventh International Conference of the "Fondation Le Pré Vert", Rüschlikon, Zürich, 1958.

Edwards, M. 1980. "Economics of home activities", in *Australian Journal of Social Issues* (Haymarket), Feb. 1980, pp. 5-17.

Eisner, R. 1978. "Total incomes in the United States, 1959 and 1969", in *Review of Income and Wealth* (New Haven, Conn.), March 1978, pp. 41-70.

Ferber, M.A. 1975. "A note on 'Household production and national production: An improvement of the record' by M. Weinrobe, 1974", in *Review of Income and Wealth* (New Haven, Conn.), Vol. 21, pp. 251-2.

————; Birnbaum, B.G. 1977. "The new home economics: Retrospects and prospects", in *Journal of Consumer Research* (Worcester, Mass.), Vol. 4, No. 1, pp. 19-29.

————; ————. 1980. "Housework: Priceless or valueless?", in *Review of Income and Wealth* (New Haven, Conn.), Dec. 1980, pp. 387-400.

Finland, Ministry of Social Affairs and Health, Research Department. 1980-81. *Housework study*. Official Statistics of Finland, Special Social Studies, XXXII, 71, 4 parts. Helsinki.

Firebaugh, F.M.; Deacon, R.E. 1980. "Contribution of women to development of the family and the economy", in C. Hefferan (ed.): *The household as producer: A look beyond the market*, op. cit., pp. 57-71.

Fourastié, J. 1965. *Les 40.000 heures*. Paris, Laffont.

Fürst, H. [1956]. *Einkommen, Nachfrage, Produktion und Konsum des privaten Haushalts in der Volkswirtschaft*. Stuttgart, Kohlhammer.

Gage, M.G. 1960. *The work load and its value for 50 homemakers in Tompkins County, New York*. Doctoral dissertation. Ithaca, N.Y., Cornell University.

————. 1965. "The homemaker, her work and the law", in *Case and Comment* (Rochester, N.Y.), Jan.-Feb. 1965, pp. 28-31.

Galbraith, J.K. 1973. *Economics and the public purpose*. Boston, Houghton Mifflin.

Gauger, W.H.; Walker, K.E. 1980. *The dollar value of household work*. New York State College of Human Ecology, Information bulletin 60, revised. Ithaca, N.Y., Cornell University.

General Electric Company. 1952. *The homemaking habits of the working wife*. New York.

Gerner, J.; Mitchell, O.; Zick, C. 1980. *Cross-substitution effects, selectivity and family labor supply*. Paper presented at the September 1980 meeting of the Econometric Society, Denver, Col. Mimeographed.

Girard, A. 1958. "Le budget-temps de la femme mariée, dans les agglomérations urbaines", in *Population* (Paris), Oct.-Dec. 1958.

Goldschmidt-Clermont, L. 1952. "L'importance économique du travail domestique et ses liens avec l'économie nationale américaine", in *Revue de l'Institut de Sociologie* (Brussels), Jan.-Mar., 1952, pp. 57-71.

Gramm, W.L. 1974. "The demand for the wife's non-market time", in *Southern Economic Journal* (Chapel Hill, N.C.), July 1974, pp. 124-133.

———. 1975. "Household utility maximization and the working wife", in *American Economic Review* (Nashville, Tenn.), March 1975, pp. 90-100.

Griffiths, M.W. 1976. "How much is a woman worth? The American public policy", in J.R. Chapman (ed.): *Economic independence for women: The foundation for equal rights*, op. cit., pp. 23-38.

Gronau, R. 1973a. "The intrafamily allocation of time: The value of the housewives time", in *American Economic Review* (Nashville, Tenn.), Sept. 1973, pp. 634-651.

———. 1973b. "The measurement of output of the non-market sector: The evaluation of housewives' time", in M. Moss (ed.): *The measurement of economic and social performance*, op. cit., pp. 163-190.

———. 1973c. "The effect of children on the housewife's value of time", in T.W. Schultz (ed.): *New economic approaches to fertility*, op. cit., pp. 168-199.

———. 1976. *Who is the main family breadwinner? The wife's contribution to full income*. Research Paper 148. Stanford, Calif., National Bureau of Economic Research. Mimeographed.

———. 1977. "Leisure, home production and work: The allocation of time revisited", in *Journal of Political Economy* (Chicago), Dec. 1977, pp. 1099-1123.

———. 1980. "Home production: A forgotten industry", in *Review of Economics and Statistics* (Cambridge, Mass.), Aug. 1980, pp. 408-416.

Hauserman, N.R.; Fethke, C. 1978. "Valuation of a homemaker's services", in *Trial Lawyer's Guide* (Wilmette, Ill.), Fall 1978, pp. 249-266.

Hawrylyshyn, O. 1976. "The value of household services: A survey of empirical estimates", in *Review of Income and Wealth* (New Haven, Conn.), June 1976, pp. 101-131.

———. 1977. "Towards a definition of non-market activities", in *Review of Income and Wealth* (New Haven, Conn.), March 1977, pp. 79-96.

Heckman, J.J. 1974. "Shadow prices, market wages and labor supply", in *Econometrica* (Evanston, Ill.), July 1974, pp. 679-694.

Hefferan, C. (ed.). 1980. *The household as producer: A look beyond the market*. Proceedings of a workshop sponsored by the family economics — home management section of the American Home Economics Association, St Charles, Mo., 21-23 June 1979. Washington, DC, American Home Economics Association.

Hegeland, H. 1973. *Väd ar hemarbetet värt?* Stockholm, Precisa tryck.

————. 1975. *Barn, kvinnor, hemarbete*. Borås.

Hershlag, Z.Y. 1960. "The case of unpaid domestic service", in *Economia internazionale* (Genoa), Feb. 1960, pp. 25-41.

Hirsch, E. 1959. Le "do-it-yourself" dans le cadre de la structure économique et sociale en Amérique", in *Le "do-it-yourself" et le commerce*, op. cit., pp. 29-40.

Honkanen, M. 1967. "Kotitaloustyön hinnoitelun perusteista", in *Kotitalous* (Helsinki), Vol. 31, No. 5, pp. 173-178.

Japan, Economic Council, Net National Welfare Measurement Committee. 1973. *Measuring net national welfare in Japan*. Tokyo.

Japan, Supreme Court. 1975. "Decision Hanrei Jiho", in *Judicial Decisions Review* (Tokyo).

Kamil, S.C.W. (ed.). 1980. *De plaats van de huishoudvoering tussen individu en samenleving: De invloed van interne en externe determinanten op structuurveranderingen in de huishouding*. Proceedings of a symposium, Wageningen, 4-5 Oct. 1979. Wageningen, Landbouwhogeschool, Vakgroep Huishoudkunde.

Kendé, P. 1978. "Les biens et les services autoproduits dans la consommation des ménages français", in A. Michel (ed.): *Les femmes dans la société marchande*, op. cit., pp. 225-244.

Kendrick, J.W. 1977. *Expanding imputed values in the national income and product accounts*. Paper presented at the 15th Annual Conference of the International Association for Research in Income and Wealth, University of York, 19-25 Aug. 1977. Mimeographed.

Kilpiö, E. 1981a. "The concept of unpaid housework and the determination of its value", in Finland, Ministry of Social Affairs and Health, Research Department: *Housework study*, op. cit., part I.

————. 1981b. "Description of the study and sample", in Finland, Ministry of Social Affairs and Health, Research Department: *Housework study*, op. cit., part II.

Kneeland, H. 1929. "Woman's economic contribution in the home", in *Annals of the American Academy of Political and Social Sciences* (Philadelphia, Pa.), May 1929, pp. 33-40.

Kravis, I.B. 1957. "The scope of economic activity in international comparison", in National Bureau of Economic Research: *Problems in the international comparison of economic accounts*, op. cit., pp. 349-377.

Kredietbank. 1975. "La femme dans l'économie", in *Bulletin hebdomadaire* (Brussels), 21 Feb. 1975, pp. 1-10.

Kreps, J.M. 1971. *Sex in the marketplace: American women at work*. Baltimore, J. Hopkins University Press.

Kuznets, S. 1941. *National income and its composition, 1919-1938*. National Bureau of Economic Research, Publication No. 40, 2 Vol. New York.

————. 1946. *National income: A summary of findings.* New York, National Bureau of Economic Research.

Kyrk, H. 1953. *The family in the American economy.* Chicago, University of Chicago Press.

Lacasse, F.D. 1971. *Women at home: The cost to the Canadian economy of the withdrawal from the labour force of a major proportion of the female population.* Studies of the Royal Commission on the Status of Women in Canada, No. 2, Ottawa, Information Canada.

Lancaster, K.J. 1966. "A new approach to consumer theory", in *Journal of Political Economy* (Chicago), Apr. 1966, pp. 132-157.

Lecoultre, D. 1976. "La valeur économique du travail non-rémunéré des femmes", in *Women at work in the labour force and at home,* op. cit., pp. 48-65.

Leibowitz, A. 1974. *Production within the household.* National Bureau of Economic Research, Working Paper No. 27. New York.

Lemel, Y. 1974. *Budgets-temps des citadins.* Institut National de la Statistique et des Etudes économiques, Série M, Ménages, No. 33. Paris.

Lindahl, E.; Dahlgren, E.; Kock, K. 1937. *National income of Sweden, 1861-1930* (in two parts). Vol. III of: *Wages, cost of living and national income in Sweden, 1860-1930,* by the staff of the Institute for Social Sciences, University of Stockholm. Stockholm Economic Studies, No. 5a and 5b. Stockholm, Norstedt and Söner.

Lindberg, V. 1943. "Suomen kansantulo vuosina 1926-1938", in *Suomen Pankin Suhdannetutkimusaston Julkaisuja* (Helsinki), Series B, No. 1.

Lindgren, J. 1974. *Kotitaloustyön arvo: Työaikatutkimukseen perustwa arviointiyritys.* Helsinki, Population Research Institute.

Lloyd, C.B. (ed.). 1975. *Sex, discrimination and the division of labor.* Columbia studies in economics, No. 8. New York, Columbia University Press.

Machlup, F. 1962. *The production and distribution of knowledge in the United States.* Princeton, Princeton University Press.

Manning, S.L. 1968. *Time use in household tasks by Indiana families.* Purdue University Agricultural Experiment Station, Research bulletin No. 837. Lafayette, Ind.

Matolcsky, M.; Varga, S. 1938. *The national income of Hungary 1924/25 – 1936/37.* London, King and Son.

Maurice, R. (ed.). 1969. *National accounts statistics: Sources and methods.* London, Central Statistical Office.

Mertens, M. 1965. "La valeur économique du travail ménager", in *Documents CEPESS* (Brussels, Centre d'Etudes politiques, économiques et sociales), Vol. 4, No. 2, pp. 100-106.

Michael, R.T.; Becker, G.S. 1973. "On the new theory of consumer behavior", in *Swedish Journal of Economics* (Stockholm), Dec. 1973, pp. 378-396.

Michel, A. 1976. "La relation profession – travail non-rémunéré de la femme, source d'inégalité de traitement: Problèmes et approches dans les pays industrialisés", in *Women at work in the labour force and at home*, op. cit., pp. 66-87.

—— (ed.). 1978. *Les femmes dans la société marchande*. Papers presented at the colloquium on "L'économie et la sociologie de la famille: La production domestique non-marchande", Royaumont, France, 2-6 January 1977. Paris, Presses Universitaires de France.

Mincer, J. 1962. "Labor force participation of married women: A study of labor supply", in *National Bureau of Economic Research: Aspects of labor economics*, op. cit., pp. 63-105.

Mitchell, W.; King, W.I.; Macaulay, F.R.; Knauth, O.W. 1921. *Income in the United States: Its amount and distribution, 1909-1919*. National Bureau of Economic Research, publication No. 1, Vol. I., summary. New York, Harcourt, Brace & Co.

Morgan, J.N. 1978. "Aspects quantitatifs de la production non-marchande dans les familles américaines", in A. Michel (ed.): *Les femmes dans la société marchande*, op. cit., pp. 205-223.

——; David, M.H.; Cohen, W.J.; Brazer, H.E. 1962. *Income and welfare in the United States*. A study by the Survey Research Center, Institute for Social Research, University of Michigan. New York, McGraw Hill.

——; Sirageldin, I.; Baerwaldt, N. 1966. *Productive Americans: A study of how individuals contribute to economic progress*. Survey Research Center, University of Michigan, monograph 43. Ann Arbor, Mich.

Moss, M. (ed.). 1973. *The measurement of economic and social performance*. Studies in income and wealth, Vol. 38, by the Conference on Research in Income and Wealth, National Bureau of Economic Research. New York, Columbia University Press.

Muellbauer, J. 1974. "Household production theory, quality and the hedonic technique", in *American Economic Review* (Nashville, Tenn.), Dec. 1974, pp. 977-994.

Murphy, M. 1976. "The value of time spent in home production", in *American Journal of Economics and Sociology* (New York), Apr. 1976, pp. 191-197.

——. 1978. "The value of non-market household production: Opportunity cost versus market cost estimates", in *Review of Income and Wealth* (New Haven, Conn.), Sep. 1978, pp. 243-255.

——. 1979. *Conceptual and theoretical issues, and methodologies of time valuation*. Paper presented at the fifth Annual Convention of the Eastern Economic Association, Boston, Mass., May 11, 1979. Mimeographed.

——. 1980. "The measurement and valuation of non-market economic activities", in C. Hefferan (ed.): *The household as producer: A look beyond the market*, op. cit., pp. 139-194.

Muth, R.F. 1966. "Household production and consumer demand functions", in *Econometrica* (Evanston, Ill.), July 1966, pp. 699-708.

National Bureau of Economic Research. 1957. *Problems in the international comparison of economic accounts*. Report to the Conference on Research in Income and Wealth, New York, October 1954. Studies in income and wealth, Vol. 20. Princeton, Princeton University Press.

————. 1962. *Aspects of labor economics*. A conference of the Universities/National Bureau Committee for Economic Research. National Bureau of Economic Research, Special conference series, No. 14. Princeton, Princeton University Press.

————. 1972. *Economic research: Retrospect and prospect*. Fiftieth anniversary colloquia. Seven volumes; General series, No. 96. New York, Columbia University Press.

Nederlandse Gezinsraad. 1972. *De economische waarde van het voeren van een gezinshuishouding*. The Hague. Mimeographed.

Nerlove, M. 1974. "Household and economy: Toward a new theory of population and economic growth", in *Journal of Political Economy* (Chicago), Vol. 82, No. 2, part II, Mar./Apr. 1974, pp. 200-233.

Nordhaus, W.; Tobin, J. 1972. "Is growth obsolete?", in National Bureau of Economic Research: *Economic research: Retrospect and prospect*, Vol. 5, *Economic growth*, pp. 1-80.

Norge, Statistiske Sentralbyra. 1948. *Nasjonalinntekten i Norge 1935-1943*. Oslo.

Ohlsson, I. 1953. *On national accounting*. Stockholm, Konjunkturinstitutet.

Owen, J.D. 1971. "The demand for leisure", in *Journal of Political Economy* (Chicago), Jan.-Feb. 1971, pp. 56-76.

Peterson, R.D. 1978. "Problems in estimating the value of household services", in *American Journal of Economics and Sociology* (New York), Apr. 1978, pp. 145-148.

Pollak, R.A.; Wachter, M.L. 1975. "The relevance of the household production function and its implications for the allocation of time," in *Journal of Political Economy* (Chicago), Apr. 1975, pp. 255-277.

————; ————. 1977. "Reply: Pollak and Wachter on the household production approach", in *Journal of Political Economy* (Chicago), Oct. 1977, pp. 1083-1086.

Proulx, M. 1978. *Cinq millions de femmes: Une étude de la femme canadienne au foyer*. Conseil Consultatif de la situation de la femme: La femme et le travail. Ottawa. Mimeographed.

Pyun, C.S. 1969. "The monetary value of a housewife: An economic analysis for use in litigation", in *American Journal of Economics and Sociology* (New York), July 1969, pp. 271-284.

Reid, M.G. 1934. *Economics of household production*. New York, Wiley and Sons.

———. 1947. "The economic contribution of homemakers", in *Annals of the American Academy of Political and Social Sciences* (Philadelphia, Pa.), May 1947, pp. 61-69.

Robinson, J. 1977. *How Americans use time: A social-psychological analysis of behavior*. New York, Praeger.

Rosen, H.S. 1974. "The monetary value of a housewife: A replacement cost approach", in *American Journal of Economics and Sociology* (New York), Vol. 33, No. 1, pp. 65-73.

Ruggles, R.; Ruggles, N. 1975. *The measurement of economic and social performance*. Paper for the fourteenth General Conference of the International Association for Research in Income and Wealth.

Santos, F.P. 1975. "The economics of marital status", in C.B. Lloyd (ed.): *Sex, discrimination and the division of labor*, op. cit., pp. 244-268.

Saunders, C.T. 1976. *The feasibility of welfare-oriented measures to complement the national accounts and balances*. Economic statistics, system of national accounts and balances. United Nations Economic and Social Council, Statistical Commission, 19th session, New Delhi, 8-19 November 1976. (Report of the Secretary-General; E/CN/477; 17 Feb. 1976)

Schacht, J. 1979. *Bemessung und Bewertung des Naturalunterhaltes in der Doppelverdienerehe*. Dissertation zur Erlangung des Doktorgrades der Juristischen Fakultät der Georg-August-Universität zu Göttingen.

Schultz, T.W. (ed.). 1973. "New economic approaches to fertility", in *Journal of Political Economy* (Chicago), Vol. 81, No. 2, part II, Mar.-Apr. 1973, supp.. Proceedings of a conference, 8-9 June 1972, sponsored by National Bureau of Economic Research and Population Council.

Schulz-Borck, H. 1975. "Was ist eine Hausfrau wert?", in *Verbraucherdienst*, Ausg. B./20, No. 4, pp. 81-87.

Scott, A.C. 1972. "The value of housework: For love or money", in *Ms Magazine*, July 1972.

Shamseddine, A.H. 1968. "GNP imputations of the value of housewives' services", in *Economic and Business Bulletin*(Philadelphia, Pa.), Summer 1968, pp. 52-61.

Sirageldin, I.A.H. 1969. *Non-market components of national income*. Survey Research Center, Institute for Social Research, University of Michigan; ISR code number 2582. Ann Arbor, Mich.

Smith, J. (ed.). 1980. *Female labor supply: Theory and estimation*. Princeton, Princeton University Press.

Stigler, G.I. 1946. *Domestic servants in the United States, 1900-1940*. National Bureau of Economic Research, Occasional paper No. 24. New York.

Stübler, E. et al. 1967. "Beiträge zur Arbeitsbewertung in hauswirtschaftlichen Tätigkeitsbereichen", in *Hauswirtschaft und Wissenschaft* (Münich), No. 3, 1967.

Suviranta, A.; Heinonen, M. 1980. "The value of unsalaried home care of children under the age of seven in 1979", in Finland, Ministry of Social Affairs and Health, Research Department: *Housework study*, op. cit., part III.

———; Mynttinen, A. 1981. "The value of unpaid housecleaning in 1980", in Finland, Ministry of Social Affairs and Health, Research Department: *Housework study*, op. cit., part IV.

Sullerot, E. 1965. *La vie des femmes*. Collection "Femmes". Paris, Gonthier.

Thorne, B. (ed.). 1981. *Rethinking the family: Some feminist questions*. New York.

"Time in economic life". 1973. *Quarterly Journal of Economics* (Cambridge, Mass.), Nov. 1973, pp. 627-675.

Vickery, C. 1978. "The time-poor: A new look at poverty", in *Journal of Human Resources* (Madison, Wisc.), Winter 1978, pp. 27-48.

Wales, T.J.; Woodland, A.D. 1977. "Estimation of the allocation of time for work, leisure and housework", in *Econometrica* (Evanston, Ill.), Jan. 1977, pp. 115-132.

Walker, K.E. 1955. *Homemaking work units for New York State households* Doctoral dissertation. Ithaca, N.Y., Cornell University.

———. 1958. *Homemaking work units*. Cornell University, Miscellaneous bulletin No. 28. Ithaca, N.Y.

———. 1978. *Valuing household production: Its importance and problems*. Paper presented at the Southwestern Regional Association of Family Economics/Home Management Conference on "Measuring and managing home production", February 1, 1978. Mimeographed.

———. 1980a. "Time measurement and the value of non-market household production", in C. Hefferan (ed.): *The household as producer: A look beyond the market*, op. cit., pp. 119-138.

———. 1980b. "A quantitative measure of productive household activities: Time-use in families with children", in S.C.W. Kamil (ed.): *De plaats van de huishoudvoering tussen individu en samenleving*, op. cit., pp. 22-41.

———; Gauger, W.H. 1973a. *The dollar value of household work*. Cornell University, New York State College of Human Ecology, Information bulletin No. 60. Ithaca, N.Y.

———; ———. 1973b. "Time and its dollar value in household work", in *Family Economics Review* (Hyattsville, Md.), Fall 1973, pp. 8-13.

———; Sanik, M.M. 1978. "The potential for measurement of nonmarket household production with time-use data", Paper presented at the ninth World Congress of Sociology, Uppsala, August 1978. Mimeographed.

———; Woods, M.E. 1976. *Time use: A measure of household production of family goods and services*. Washington, DC, Center for the Family, American Home Economics Association.

Warren, J. 1938. *Use of time in its relation to home management*. Doctoral dissertation. Ithaca, N.Y., Cornell University.

———. 1940. *Use of time in its relation to home management*. Cornell University, Agricultural Experiment Station Bulletin No. 734. Ithaca, N.Y.

Weinrobe, M. 1974. "Household production and national production: An improvement of the record", in *Review of Income and Wealth* (New Haven, Conn.), Mar. 1974, pp. 89-102.

———. 1975. "Reply to M.A. Ferber", in *Review of Income and Wealth* (New Haven, Conn.), Vol. 21, pp. 252-253.

Weisbrod, B.A. 1961. *Economics of public health: Measuring the economic impact of disease*. Philadelphia, Pa., University of Pennsylvania Press.

Wiegand, E. 1953. *Comparative use of time of farm and city full-time homemakers, and homemakers in the labor force in relation to home management*. Doctoral dissertation. Ithaca, N.Y., Cornell University.

———. 1954. *Use of time by full-time and part-time homemakers in relation to home management*. Cornell University, Agricultural Experiment Station Memoir No. 330. Ithaca, N.Y.

Women at work in the labour force and at home. 1976. Working papers prepared for Research Symposium on Women and Decision Making: A Social Policy Priority, Geneva, 17-19 November 1975. Research series, No. 22. Geneva, International Institute for Labour Studies.